Learn Python

The Ultimate Beginner's Guide to Python for Machine Learning and Deep Learning Using scikit-learn and tensorflow with Hands-On Projects

Zed Fast

Table of Contents

Introduction 1
Chapter 1: Fundamentals of Machine Learning 5
Basic Concepts of Machine Learning 7
Basic Machine Learning Terminologies 13
Types of Machine Learning Models 21
Machine Learning in Practice 30
Importance of Machine-Learning.................................. 31
Chapter 2: Machine Learning Algorithms..................... 35
Supervised Machine Learning Algorithms 36
Unsupervised Machine Learning Algorithms 38
Semi-Supervised Machine Learning Algorithms 39
Reinforcement Machine Learning Algorithms.................. 40
Pruning 61
The Kernel Trick 67
Chapter 3: Data Pre-processing and Creation of Training
Data Set 71
Overview of Data Preprocessing 71
Steps of Data Pre-Processing 76
Challenges of Categorical Data 83
Encoding Categorical Data 84
Building Data Pipeline for Machine Learning................... 91
Chapter 4: Scikit-Learn 115
Prerequisites for Application of Scikit-Learn Library 117
Installing Scikit-Learn 122
Data Exploration 127
Data Visualization.. 129
Data Pre-Processing.. 132
Creating Training and Test Subsets.............................. 134
Building the Machine Learning Model............................ 137
Chapter 5: Training Neural Network with Tensorflow. 143
Neural Network 145
Fundamentals of Neural Network 147
Training a Neural Network Using TensorFlow 149
Configuring the Layers 154
Compiling the Model 155
Conclusion... 175

Introduction

Congratulations on purchasing *Learn Python: The Ultimate Beginner's Guide to Python for Machine Learning and Deep Learning Using scikit-learn and tensorflow with Hands on Projects* and thank you for doing so.

The following chapters will discuss the core concepts of "Machine Learning" models that are being developed and advanced using Python programming language. This book will provide you overarching guidance on how you can use Python to develop machine learning models using Scikit-Learn and TensorFlow machine learning libraries. You will start this book with gaining a solid understanding of the basics of the machine learning technology and types of machine learning models with an emphasis on the deep learning model called "Artificial Neural Network." It is important to master the concepts of machine learning technology and learn how researchers are breaking the boundaries of data science to mimic human intelligence in machines using a wide variety of learning algorithms. The power of machine learning technology has already started to manifest in our environment to enhance the usability of our household objects.

In Chapter 2 titled, "Machine Learning Algorithms," you will learn the nuances of "12 of the most popular machine learning algorithms," in a very easy to understand language that requires no background in Python coding language and in fact might spike your interest in this field of research. You will also learn the fundamental machine learning algorithms in great detail, namely, supervised, unsupervised, and reinforcement machine learning algorithms that serve as the skeleton of hundreds of machine learning algorithms being developed everyday.

In Chapter 3 titled, "Data pre-processing and Creation of training data set," you will learn all about the most time consuming and critical aspect of developing a machine learning model i.e. Data pre-processing and splitting the processed data set into training and testing subsets. A detailed step by step description of different stages involved in the process of creating training data set has been provided to give you an end to end understanding of this most critical aspect of the development of machine learning algorithms.

In chapter 4, titled "Scikit-Learn," we deep dive into the functioning of Scikit-Learn library along with the pre-requisites required to develop machine learning model using Scikit-Learn library. A detailed walkthrough with an open source database using illustrations and actual Python code that you can try hands on by following the instructions in this book. There is no better way to learn than to actually get your hands dirty and get real experience of the task. There is also guidance provided on resolving nonlinear issues with "k-nearest neighbor" and "kernel trick algorithms" in this book.

You will learn the entire process of creating of Neural Network models on TensorFlow machine learning platform, using open source data set as example, along with the actual Python code used for the development, in the chapter 5, titled "Training Neural Network with TensorFlow." Neural Networks are characterized by a "single neuron like entity of the machine that is capable of learning the expected output for a given input from training data sets." TensorFlow is built on Python and touted as a simple and flexible architecture that supports development of machine learning ideas from "concept to code to state-of-the-art models and to publication" in short period of time. Finally, as an added bonus you will learn some Python tips and tricks to take your machine learning programming game to the next level. So, breathe in, breathe out, and let's begin!

There are plenty of books on this subject on the market, thanks again for choosing this one! Every effort was made to ensure it is full of as much useful information as possible, please enjoy!

Chapter 1: Fundamentals of Machine Learning

The concept of Artificial Intelligence technology stems from the idea that machines are capable of human like intelligence and can mimic human thought processing and learning capabilities, to adapt to new inputs and perform tasks without requiring human assistance. Machine learning is integral to the concept of artificial intelligence. Machine learning technology (ML) is referred to the concept of Artificial Intelligence technology that focuses primarily on the engineered capability of machines to explicitly learn and self train, by identifying data patterns to improve upon the underlying algorithm and make independent decisions with no human intervention." In 1959, pioneering computer gaming and artificial intelligence expert, Arthur Samuel, coined the term "machine learning" during his tenure at IBM.

Machine learning hypothesizes that modern day computers have an ability to be trained using targeted training data sets that can be easily customized to develop desired functionalities. Machine learning is driven by the pattern recognition technique where the machine records and revisits past interactions and results that are deemed in alignment with its current situation. Given the fact that machines are required to process endless amount of data, with new data always pouring in, they must be equipped to adapt to the new data without needing to be programmed by a human, which speaks to the iterative aspect of ML.

Now the topic of machine learning is so "hot" that the academia, business world and the scientific community have their own take on its definition. Here are some of the widely accepted definitions from select highly reputed sources:

- *"Machine learning is the science of getting computers to act without being explicitly programmed."* – Stanford University
- *"The field of Machine Learning seeks to answer the question, how can we build computer systems that automatically improve with experience, and what are the fundamental laws that govern all learning processes?"* – Carnegie Mellon University

- *"Machine learning algorithms can figure out how to perform important tasks by generalizing from examples."* – University of Washington
- *"Machine Learning at its most basic is the practice of using algorithms to parse data, learn from it, and then make a determination or prediction about something in the world."* – Nvidia
- *"Machine learning is based on algorithms that can learn from data without relying on rules-based programming."* – McKinsey.

Basic Concepts of Machine Learning

The biggest draw of machine learning is the engineered capability of the system to learn programs from the data automatically instead of manually constructing the program for the machine. Over the last decade the use of machine learning algorithms expanded from computer science to the industrial world. Machine learning algorithms are capable of generalizing tasks to execute them iteratively. The process of developing specific programs for specific tasks costs a lot of time and money, but occasionally it's just impossible to achieve. On the other hand, ML programming is often feasible and tends to be much more cost effective. The use of machine learning in tackling ambitious issues of widespread importance such as global warming and depleting underground water levels is promising with massive collection of relevant data.

"A breakthrough in machine learning would be worth ten Microsofts."
– Bill Gates

A number of types of machine learning exist today but the concept of machine learning largely boils down to three components "representation," "evaluation" and "optimization." Here are some of the standard concepts that are applicable to all of them:

Representation

Machine learning models are incapable of directly hearing, seeing or sensing input examples. Therefore, a data representation is required to supply the model with a useful vantage point into the key qualities of the data. To be able to successfully train a machine learning model selection of key features that best represent the data is very important. "Representation" simply refers to the act of "representing" data points to computer in a language that it understands using a set of classifiers. A classifier can be defined as "a system that inputs a vector of discrete and or continuous feature values and outputs a single discrete value called class." For a model to learn from the represented data the training data set or the "hypothesis space" must contain desired classifier that you want the models to be trained on. Any classifiers that are external to the hypothesis space cannot be learned by the model.

The data features used to represent the input are very critical to the machine learning process. The data features are so important to the development of desired machine learning model that it can easily be the difference between successful and failed machine learning projects. A training data set containing multiple independent "features" that are well correlated with the "class" can make the machine learning much smoother. On the other hand, class containing complex features may not be easy to learn from for the machine. This often requires the raw data to be processed so that desired features can be constructed from it, to be leveraged for the ML model. The process of deriving features from raw data tends to be the most time consuming and laborious part the ML project. It is also considered the most creative and interesting part of the project where intuition and trial and error play just as important role as the technical requirements.

The process of ML is not a "one shot process" of developing a training data set and executing it instead it is an iterative process that requires analysis of the post run output, followed by modification of the training data set and then repeating the whole process all over again. Another reason for the extensive time and effort required to engineer the training data set is domain specificity. Training data set for an e-commerce platform to generate predictions based on consumer behavior analysis will be very different from the training data set required to develop a self driving car. However, the actual machine learning process remains largely the same across industrial domains. No wonder, a lot of research is being done to automate the feature engineering process.

Evaluation

Essentially the process of judging multiple hypothesis or models to choose one model over another is referred to as an evaluation. To be able to differentiate between useful classifiers from the vague ones an "evaluation function" is required. The evaluation function is also called as "objective," "utility" or "scoring" function. The machine learning algorithm has its own internal evaluation function which tends to be different from the external evaluation function used by the researchers to optimize the classifier. Usually the evaluation function is defined prior to the selection of the data representation tool, as the first step of the project. For example, the machine learning model for self driving car has the feature for identification of pedestrians in its vicinity at near zero false negatives and a low false positive as an evaluation function and the pre-existing condition that needs to be "represented" using applicable data features.

Optimization

The process of searching the space of presented models to achieve better evaluations or highest scoring classifier is called as "optimization." For algorithms with more than one optimum classifier, the selection of optimization technique is very critical in determination of the classifier produced and to achieve a more efficient learning model. A variety of off-the-shelf optimizers are available in the market to kick start new machine learning models before eventually replacing them with custom designed optimizers.

Table 1. The three components of learning algorithms.

Representation	Evaluation	Optimization
Instances	Accuracy/Error rate	Combinatorial optimization
K-nearest neighbor	Precision and recall	Greedy search
Support vector machines	Squared error	Beam search
Hyperplanes	Likelihood	Branch-and-bound
Naive Bayes	Posterior probability	Continuous optimization
Logistic regression	Information gain	Unconstrained
Decision trees	K-L divergence	Gradient descent
Sets of rules	Cost/Utility	Conjugate gradient
Propositional rules	Margin	Quasi-Newton methods
Logic programs		Constrained
Neural networks		Linear programming
Graphical models		Quadratic programming
Bayesian networks		
Conditional random fields		

Basic Machine Learning Terminologies

Agent – In context of reinforcement learning, an agent refers to "the entity that uses a policy to maximize expected return gained from transitioning between states of the environment."

Boosting – Boosting can be defined as "a machine learning technique that iteratively combines a set of simple and not very accurate classifiers (referred to as weak classifiers) into a classifier with high accuracy (a strong classifier) by up-weighting the examples that the model is currently misclassifying."

Candidate generation – The phase of selecting the "first set of recommendations" by a recommendation system is referred to as candidate generation. For example, a book library can offer 500,000 titles. This technique will produce a subset of few 100 books meeting the needs of a particular user and can be refined further to an even smaller set as needed.

Categorical Data – Data features boasting a "discrete set of possible values" is called as categorical data. For example, a "categorical feature" labeled car style can have an unconnected set of multiple possible values including sedan, coupe, SUV.

Checkpoint – Checkpoint can be defined as "The data that can capture the state of the variables of a learning model particular moment in time." With the use of checkpoints, training can be carried out across multiple sessions and model weights or scores can be exported.

Class – Class can be defined as "one of a set of listed target values for a given label." For example, a machine learning model designed to detect "spam" will have two classes, namely, "spam" and "not spam."

Classification model – The type of ML model used to "distinguish between two or more discrete classes of data" is referred to as classification model. For example, a classification model for identification of dog breeds could assess whether the dog picture used as input is Labrador, Schnauzer, German Shepherd, Beagle and so on.

Collaborative filtering – The process of generating predictions for a particular user based on the shared interests of a group of similar users is called as collaborative filtering.

Continuous feature – It is defined as a "floating-point feature with an infinite range of possible values."

Discrete feature – It is defined as a "rigid feature with a finite set of possible values."

Discriminator – "The system that determines whether the input examples are real or fake" is called as discriminator.

Down-sampling – The process of Down-sampling refers to "the act of reducing the amount of information contained in a feature or using a disproportionately low percentage of over-represented class examples in order to train the learning model more efficiently."

Dynamic model – A learning model that is continuously receiving input data to be trained in a continuous manner is called as dynamic model.

Ensemble – "The set of predictions generated by

merging predictions of multiple models" is called as ensemble.

Environment – The term 'environment' used in context of reinforcement machine learning constitutes "the world that contains the agent and allows the agent to observe that world's state."

Episode – The term episode used in context of reinforcement machine learning constitutes "every iterative attempt made by the agent to learn from its environment."

Feature – "An input data variable that is used in generating predictions" is called as a feature.

Feature engineering – Feature engineering can be defined as "the process of determining which features might be useful in training a model, and then converting raw data from log files and other sources into said features."

Feature extraction – Feature extraction can be defined as "the process of Retrieving intermediate feature representations calculated by an unsupervised or pre-trained model for use in another model as input."

Few-shot learning - Few-shot learning can be defined as "a machine learning approach, often used for object classification, designed to learn effective classifiers from only a small number of training examples."

Fine tuning – The process of "performing a secondary optimization to adjust the parameters of an already trained model to fit a new problem" is called as fine tuning. It is widely used to refit the weights of a "trained unsupervised model" to a "supervised model."

Generalization – "The ability of the machine learning model to make correct predictions on new, previously unseen data as opposed to the data used to train the model" is called as generalization.

Inference – In context of ML, inference can be defined as "the process of making predictions by applying the trained model to unlabeled examples."

Label – In context of machine learning (supervised), the "answer" or "result" part of an example is called as label.

A labeled data set can constitute single or multiple features and corresponding labels for every example. For example, in a house data set, the features could include the year built, number of bedrooms and bathrooms, while the label can be the "house's price."

Linear model – Linear model is defined as "a model that assigns one weight per feature to make predictions."

Loss – In context of machine learning, loss refers to the "measure of how far the predictions are generated by the model from its label."

Matplotlib – It is "an open-source Python 2D plotting library which is used to visualize different aspects of machine learning."

Model – In context of ML, model can be defined as "the representation of what a machine learning system has learned from the training data."

NumPy – "An open-source math library that provides efficient array operations in Python."

One-shot learning – In context of ML, one-shot learning refers to "a machine learning approach designed to learn effective classifiers from a single training example, often used for object classification."

Overfitting - In context of machine learning, overfitting is referred to as "creation of a model that matches the training data so closely that the model fails to make correct predictions on new data."

Parameter – "A variable of a model that the machine learning system is able to train on its own" is called as parameter.

Pipeline – In context of ML, pipeline refers to "the infrastructure surrounding a machine learning algorithm and includes collection of data, addition of the data to training data files, training one or more models, and exporting the models to production."

Random forest – In context of machine learning, the concept of random forest pertains to "an ensemble approach for finding the decision tree that best fits the training data by developing multiple decision trees with a random selection of features."

Scaling - In context of machine learning, scaling refers to "a common feature engineering practice to tame a feature's range of values to match the range of other features in the dataset."

Sequence model - A sequence model simply refers to a model with sequential dependency on data inputs to generate a future prediction.

Under-fitting - In context of ML, under-fitting refers to "production of a ML model with poor predictive ability because the model hasn't captured the complexity of the training data."

Validation – "The process used to evaluate the quality of a machine learning model using the validation set, as part of the model training phase" is called as validation. The main goal of this process is to make sure that the performance of the ML model can be applied beyond the training set.

Types of Machine Learning Models

Deep Learning with Artificial Neural Networks

"Artificial Neural Networks" or (ANN) have been developed with an inspiration from structure of the human brain and utilizes numerous processing units like human neurons or nodes working as one. Each ANN has numerous concealed layers including an input and an output layer. These neurons are connected in a complex with one another by weighted links. A solitary neuron is capable of accepting input from various neurons. When a neuron gets activated, it casts a "weighted vote" to control the activation of the subsequent neuron that is collecting that input. An algorithm modifies these weights in accordance with the training data to optimize learning. A simple algorithm called "fire together, wire together" increases the weight between two connected neurons when the activation of either neuron leads to subsequent activation of the other neuron. "Concepts" are formed and distributed through the sub-network of shared neurons. The simplest form of neural network is comprised of a single neuron and is known as "Perceptron."

The most widely recognized ANN deal with unidirectional progression of information and are called "Feed forward ANN." However, ANN can also be used for bidirectional and cyclic progression of information to gain state equilibrium. ANNs are less dependent on prior assumptions and able to learn from prior cases by modifying the connected weights. They can be utilized with either supervised or non supervised learning. The use of supervised learning will generate correct ANN output for every input pattern. By varying the weights, the error between the target output and the output produced by ANN can be effectively minimized. For example, a type of "supervised learning algorithm" called "reinforced learning," informs the ANN whether the output it produced is correct or not in lieu of directly supplying the correct output. On the other hand, "unsupervised learning algorithm" is capable of providing variety of input pattern to the ANN which are then processed by the ANN to self explore the relationship between the provided input patterns and learn to categorize them accordingly. Artificial Neural Networks utilizing a combination of "supervised" and "unsupervised" learning are also available.

ANN is the choice of the learning model to address data driven problems with unknown or difficult to comprehend algorithm or rules, credited to their defined data structure and nonlinear computations. ANNs are capable of efficiently processing complex information and can easily withstand multi-variable data errors. Problems requiring a complete understanding of and insight into the actual process are not suitable for the ANN model, given its black box nature providing no view into the underlying process. The Python library that is most widely used to develop and evaluate deep learning models is called "Keras," which encompasses other Python libraries including "Theano" and "TensorFlow."

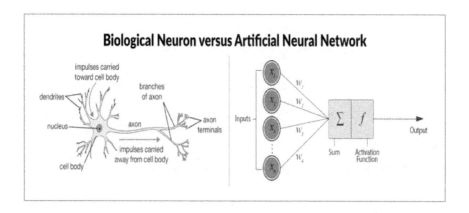

ANNs are widely used to resolve problems that require:

- **"Pattern classification"** by assigning input pattern to one of the pre-determined classes. For example, classification of land based on satellite images.

- **"Clustering,"** which is simply an unsupervised pattern classification model. For example, prediction of ecological status of water streams using defined input patterns.

- **"Function approximation or regression,"** which is capable of creating a function out of the provided set of training patterns. For example, prediction of ozone concentration in the atmosphere, estimation of amount of nitrate in groundwater and modeling water supply.

- **"Prediction,"** which utilized prior data samples in a time series to estimate the output. For example, prediction of air and water quality.

- **"Optimization,"** which is used to maximize or minimize a "cost function" subject to predefined constraints. For example, calibration of infiltration equations.

- **"Retrieval by content,"** which is capable of recalling memory even if the input is incomplete or distorted. For example, using the satellite images to produce water quality proxies.

- **"Process control,"** which seeks to keep the velocity under changing data load close to constant by changing the throttle angle. For example, engine speed control.

Genetic Algorithms

As one can gather from the name, Genetic Algorithm (GA) mimics the nature's theory of selection by transferring the traits of the fitter solutions to the "offspring" and supplanting the less fit solutions. The Genetic Algorithm will keep evolving until a desired solution of the problem is achieved. Similar to human chromosomes, every potential solution is encoded as a "binary string" of traits and each arrangement of progressive population are referred to as "generations." The original population set is produced randomly, and all superseding generations are created through the process of selection and reproduction. A specific subset of the populace is then selectively bred to produce new chromosomes. The process of selection is driven by the fitness of the individual solutions including closeness to a perfect solution and deterministic examining. The closeness to a perfect selection is frequently carried out by the "roulette selection" method leading to arbitrary selection of a parent with calculated probability based on its fitness. Then the deterministic examining allots a value to a subset of selected organism.

Conventional propagation is achieved through genetic crossover, which produces the offspring by trading chromosomes from two parents and inserting mutations in the chromosome to randomly modify some portion of the parent chromosome. The propagation doesn't happen as often as in the human world but allows introduction of new genetic material in the gene pool. Mutation is considered less important than crossover in the advancement of the search but is deemed vital in the maintenance of genetic diversity, which is the fundamental to continued evolution. In steady-state genetic algorithms, fewer fit members are superseded by the new generation, bringing about an increase in the average fitness of the model. The cycle of "reproduction and selection" is repeated until the completion criteria is met, for example, optimum fitness has been reached or all organisms are identical, and evolution is not generating new results.

By focusing only on fitness examination and not accounting for other derivatives, genetic algorithms are considered highly robust computationally and capable of can smoothly balancing load and efficacy. Another significant aspect of genetic algorithm is its capability to indirectly sample a big volume of code sequences that have actually been tested. Unlike the stochastic search techniques which cannot search through noisy and multimodal relations, genetic algorithm is able to store a whole population of solutions instead of adjusting just a single solution. Some application examples of genetic algorithms include: "forecasting air quality, calibration of the water-quality models, estimation of soil bulk density and water management systems."

Decision Trees

A machine learning decision tree can be defined as "a tree like graphical representation of the decision-making process, by taking into consideration all the conditions or factors that can influence the decision and the consequences of those decisions." Decision trees are considered one of the simplest "supervised machine learning algorithms" and has three main elements: "branch nodes" representing conditions of the data set, "edges" representing ongoing decision process and "leaf nodes" representing end of the decision. Decision trees make for an excellent predictive analysis technique with wide application in generating predictions for the values of "categorical" as well as "continuous" target variables. (Note – The very important concept of Decision Trees will be explored in detail in the next chapter of this book.)

Probabilistic Programming

"Probabilistic programming" is a high-level programming language that empower formation of probability models, with the capability to extract values from distributions and condition these values into a program. The Probabilistic programming-based learning systems are capable of making inferences from earlier knowledge, permitting decision making even in the face of uncertainty. To capture the knowledge of the target system "quantitative" and "probabilistic" terms are utilized. With adequate training, the model can be applied to explicit inquires to generate answers by means of a process called "inference."

With the use of probabilistic programming language, the probability model can also be solved automatically without any external assistance. It also supports uninterrupted access and reusability of machine learning model libraries and provides support for interactive modeling as well as formal verification. The abstraction layer within the probabilistic algorithm is paramount to nurture generic and efficient inferences, considering the fact that various Artificial Intelligence problems require the agent to process fragmented and distorted data set. Probabilistic algorithms are widely used to analyze large volumes of data to generate predictions and assist perception systems in analysis of the underlying processes. Some examples of Probabilistic programming applications are: "medical imaging," "financial predictions," "machine perception" and "weather forecasting."

The most widely used probabilistic model is called "Bayesian network," which uses "Bayesian inference" to compute probability. The Bayesian network can generate inferences in two forms. The first one is assessment of the joint probability of a specific assignment of values for every single variable in the network. While the second form is assessment of the probability of a subset of variables that have been given assignments of an alternate subset of variables. The problems pertaining to reasoning, learning, planning and perception of the system can be addressed with application of the Bayesian networks. The "Bayesian inference algorithm" is utilized in resolution of reasoning problems while the "expectation" and "maximization" algorithm can be used to address learning problems. The dynamic Bayesian networks allow for unfettered perception and decision networks which are widely used to solve planning issues.

Machine Learning in Practice

The complete process of machine learning is much more extensive than just the development and application of machine learning algorithms and can be divided into steps below:

1. Define the goals of the project taking into careful consideration all the prior knowledge and domain expertise available. Goals can easily become ambiguous since there are always additional things you want to achieve than practically possible to implement.
2. The data pre-processing and cleaning must result in a high-quality data set. This is the most critical and time-consuming step of the whole project. The larger the volume of data, the more noise it brings to the training data set which must be eradicated before feeding to the learner system.

3. Selection of appropriate learning model to meet the requirements of your project. This process tends to be rather simple given the variety types of data models available in the market.

4. Depending on the domain the machine learning model is applied to, the results may or may not require a clear understanding of the model by human experts as long as the model can successfully deliver desired results.

5. The final step is to consolidate and deploy the knowledge or information gathered from the model to be used on an industrial level.

6. The whole cycle from step 1 to 5 listed above is iteratively repeated until a result that can be used in practice is achieved.

Importance of Machine-Learning

To get a sense of how significant machine learning is in our every day lives, it is simpler to state what part of our cutting-edge way of life has not been touched by it. Each aspect of human life is being impacted by the "smart machines" intended to expand human capacities and improve efficiencies. Artificial Intelligence and machine learning technology is the focal precept of the "Fourth

Industrial Revolution," that could possibly question our thoughts regarding being "human."

Here are few reasons to help you understand the significance of machine learning in our daily lives:

- Automation of repetitive learning and revelation from data. Not at all like hardware-driven robotic automation that simply automate manual assignments, machine learning allows performance of high volume, high volume, computer-based tasks consistently and dependably.
- Machine learning algorithms are helping Artificial Intelligence to adapt to the evolving world by allowing the machine or system to learn, take note and improve up on its prior errors. Machine learning algorithm functions as a classifier or a predictor to acquire new skills and identify data pattern and structure. For example, machine learning algorithm has generated a system that can teach itself how to play chess and even how to generate product recommendations based on customer activity and behavior data. The beauty of this model is that it adapts with every new set of data.

- Machine learning has made analysis of deeper and larger data set feasible with the use of neural networks containing multiple hidden layers. Think about it, a fraud detection system with numerous concealed layers would deem a work of fantasy just a couple of years ago. With the advent of big data and unlikely to envision computer powers, a whole new world is on the horizon. Data to the machines resembles the gas to the vehicle, the more data you can add to them, faster and more accurate results will get. Deep learning models flourish with abundance of data because they gain straightforwardly from the data.

- The "deep neural networks" of the machine learning algorithms have resulted in unbelievable accuracy. For example, frequent and repeated use of smart tech like "Amazon Alexa" and "Google Search," result in increased accuracy derived from deep learning. These "deep neural networks" are also empowering our medical field. Image classification and object recognition are now capable of finding cancer on MRIs with similar accuracy as that of a highly trained radiologist.

- Artificial Intelligence is allowing for enhanced and improved use of bid data analytics in conjunction with machine learning algorithms. Data has evolved as its own currency and when algorithms are self learning it can easily become "intellectual property." The raw data is similar to a gold mine in that the more and deeper you dig, the more "gold" or valuable insight you can dig out or extract. Application of machine learning algorithms to the data can enable you to find the correct solutions quicker and makes for an upper hand. Keep in mind the best information will consistently win, despite the fact that everyone is utilizing comparative techniques.

Chapter 2: Machine Learning Algorithms

By utilizing prior computations and underlying algorithms, machines are now capable of learning from and training on their own to generate high-quality, readily reproducible decisions and results. The notion of machine learning has been around for a long time now, but latest advances in machine learning algorithms have made large data processing and analysis feasible for computers. This is achieved by applying sophisticated and complicated mathematical calculations using high speed and frequency automation. Today's advanced computing machines are able to analyze humongous information quantities quickly and deliver quicker and more precise outcomes. Companies using machine learning algorithms have increased flexibility to change the training data set to satisfy their company needs and train the machines accordingly. These tailored algorithms of machine learning enable companies to define potential hazards and possibilities for development. Typically, machine learning algorithms are used in cooperation with artificial intelligence technology and cognitive techniques to create computers extremely efficient and extremely effective in processing large quantities of information or big data and to generate extremely precise outcomes.

There are four fundamental types of machine learning algorithms available today.

Supervised Machine Learning Algorithms

Due to their ability to evaluate and apply the lessons learned from prior iterations and interactions to fresh input data set, the supervised learning algorithms are commonly used in predictive big data analysis. Based on the instructions given to effectively predict and forecast future occurrences, these algorithms can label all their ongoing runs. For instance, people can program the machine as "R" (Run), "N" (Negative) or "P" (Positive) to label its data points. The algorithm for machine learning will then label the input data as programmed and obtain data inputs with the right outputs. The algorithm will compare its own produced output to the "anticipated or correct" output, identifying future changes that can be created and fixing mistakes to make the model more precise and smarter. By using methods such as "regression," "prediction," "classification" and "ingredient boosting" to train the machine learning algorithms well, any new input data can be fed into the machine as a set of "target" data to orchestrate the learning program as desired. This "known training data set" jump starts the analytical process followed by the learning algorithm to produce an "inferred feature" that can be used to generate forecasts and predictions based on output values for future occurrences. For instance, financial institutions and banks rely strongly on monitoring machine learning algorithms to detect credit card fraud and predict the probability of a prospective credit card client failing to make their credit payments on time.

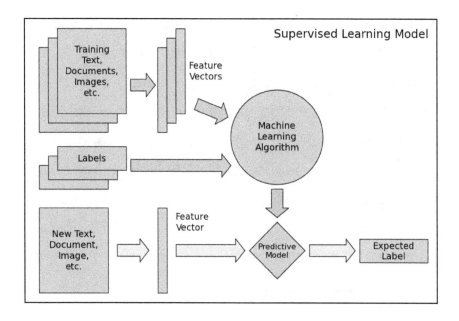

Unsupervised Machine Learning Algorithms

Companies often find themselves in a scenario where information sources are inaccessible that are needed to produce a labeled and classified training data set. Using unsupervised ML algorithms is perfect in these circumstances. Unsupervised ML algorithms are widely used to define how the machine can generate "inferred features" to elucidate a concealed construct from the stack of unlabeled and unclassified data collection. These algorithms can explore the data in order to define a structure within the data mass. Unlike the supervised machine learning algorithms, the unsupervised algorithms fail to identify the correct output, although they are just as effective as the supervised learning algorithms in investigating input data and drawing inferences. These algorithms can be used to identify information outliers, generate tailored and custom product recommendations, classify text subjects using methods such as "self-organizing maps," "singular value decomposition," and "k-means clustering." For instance, customer identification with shared shopping characteristics that can be segmented into particular groups and focused on with comparable marketing strategies and campaigns. As a result, in the online marketing world, unsupervised learning algorithms are extremely popular.

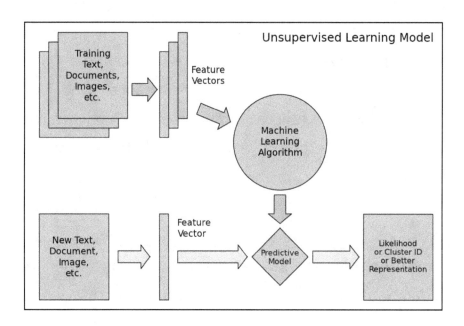

Semi-Supervised Machine Learning Algorithms

Highly versatile, the "semi-supervised machine learning algorithms" are capable of using both labeled and unlabeled information set to learn from and train themselves. These algorithms are a "hybrid" of algorithms that are supervised and unsupervised. Typically, with a small volume of labeled data, the training data set is comprised of predominantly unlabeled data. The use of analytical methods including "forecast," "regression" and "classification" in conjunction with semi-supervised learning algorithms enables the machine to considerably enhance its learning precision and training capabilities. These algorithms are commonly used in instances where it is highly resource intensive and less cost-effective for the business to generate labeled training data set from raw unlabeled data. Companies use semi-supervised learning algorithms on their systems to avoid incurring extra costs of staff and equipment. For instance, implementation for "facial recognition" technology needs a huge amount of facial data distributed across various sources of input. The raw data pre-processing, processing, classification and labeling, acquired from sources such as internet cameras, needs a lot of resources and thousands of hours of job to be used as a training data set.

Reinforcement Machine Learning Algorithms

The "reinforcement machine learning algorithms" are much more distinctive in that they learn from the environment. These algorithms conduct activities and record the outcomes of each action diligently, which would have been either a failure resulting in mistake or reward for good performance. The two primary features that differentiate the reinforcement learning algorithms are: the research method of "trial and error" and feedback loop of "delayed reward." Using a range of calculations, the computer constantly analyzes input data and sends a reinforcement signal for each right or anticipated output to ultimately optimize the end result. The algorithm develops a straightforward action and reward feedback loop to evaluate, record and learn which actions have been effective and in a shorter period of time have resulted in correct or expected output. The use of these algorithms allows the system to automatically determine optimal behaviors and maximize its efficiency within the constraints of a particular context. The reinforcement machine learning algorithms are therefore strongly used in gaming, robotics engineering and navigation systems.

The machine learning algorithms have proliferated to hundreds and thousands and counting. Here are some of the most widely used algorithms:

1. Regression

The methods of "regression" fall under the supervised machine learning category. They assist in predicting or describing a specific numeric value on the basis of the set of preceding data, such as anticipating a property's price based on preceding price data for comparable properties. Regression methods range from simple (such as "linear regression") to complex (such as "regular linear regression," "polynomial regression," "decision trees," "random forest regression" and "neural networks," among others).

The easiest technique of all is "linear regression," where the "mathematical equation of the line ($y = m * x + b$) is used to model a data set." A "linear regression" model can be trained with multiple "data pairs (x, y)" by calculating a line's position and slope that can reduce the overall distance between data points and the line. In other words, for a line that generates best approximation for the data observations, the calculation of the "slope (m)" and "y-intercept (b)" is used.

For example, using "linear regression" technique to generate predictions for the energy consumption (in kWh) of houses by collecting the age of the house, number of bedrooms, square footage area and number of installed electronic equipment. Now, we have more than one input (year built, square footage) it is possible to use "linear multi-variable regression." The underlying process is the same as "one-to - one linear regression," however, the "line" created was based on the number of variables in multi-dimensional space.

The above plot demonstrates how well the model of linear regression fits the real construction energy consumption. In case where you could gather house characteristics such as year built and square footage, but you don't understand the house's energy consumption then you are better off using the fitted line to generate approximations for the house's energy consumption.

2. Classification

The method of "classification" is another class of "supervised machine learning," which can generate predictions or explanations for a "class value." For example, this method can be used to predict the if of an online customer will actually purchase a particular product. The result generated will be reported as a yes or no response i.e. "buyer" or "not a buyer." But techniques of classification are not restricted to two classes. A classification technique, for instance, could assist to evaluate whether a specified picture includes a sedan or a SUV. The output will be three different values in this case: 1) the picture contains a sedan, 2) the picture contains a SUV, or 3) the picture does not contain either a sedan or a SUV.

"Logistic regression" is considered the easiest classification algorithm, though the term comes across as a "regression" technique but that is far from the reality. "Logistic regression" generates estimations for the likelihood of an event taking place based on single or multiple input values. For example, to generate estimation for the likelihood of a student being accepted to a specific university, a "logistic regression" will use the standardized testing scores and university testing score for a student as inputs. The generated prediction is a probability, ranging between '0' and '1,' where 1 is full assurance. For the student, if the estimated likelihood is greater than 0.5, then prediction would be that they will be accepted. If the projected probability is less than 0.5, the prediction would be that they will be denied admission.

The following graph shows the ratings of past learners as well as whether they have been accepted. Logistic regression enables creation of a line that can represent the "decision boundary."

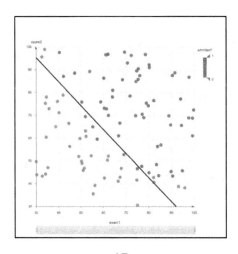

3. Clustering

We enter the category of unsupervised machine learning, with "clustering methods" because its objective is to "group or cluster observations with comparable features." Clustering methods do not use output data to train but allow the output to be defined by the algorithm. Only data visualizations can be used in clustering techniques to check the solution's quality.

"K-Means clustering," where 'K' is used to represent the number of "clusters" that the customer elects to generate and is the most common clustering method. (Note that different methods for selecting K value, such as the "elbow technique," are available.)

Steps used by K-Means clustering to process the data points:

1. The data centers are selected randomly by 'K.'
2. Assigns each data point to the nearest centers that have been randomly generated.
3. Re-calculates each cluster's center.
4. If centers do not change (or have minor change), the process will be completed.

Otherwise, we'll go back to step 2. (Set a maximum amount of iterations in advance to avoid getting stuck in an infinite loop, if the center of the cluster continues to alter.)

The following plot applies "K-Means" to a building data set. Each column in the plot shows each building's efficiency. The four measurements relate to air conditioning, heating, installed electronic appliances (refrigerators, TV) and cooking gas. For simplicity of interpretation of the results, 'K' can be set to value '2' for clustering, wherein one cluster will be selected as an efficient building group and the other cluster as an inefficient building group. You see the place of the structures on the left as well as couple of the building characteristics used as inputs on the right: installed electronic appliances and heating.

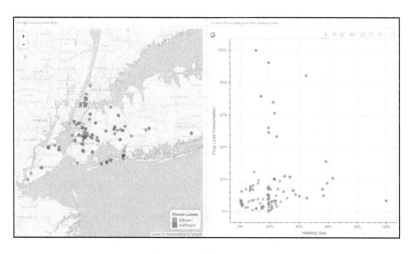

4. Dimension Reduction

As the name indicates, to extract the least significant information (sometimes redundant columns) from a data set, we use "dimensionality reduction." In practice, date sets tend to contain hundreds or even thousands of rows (also known as characteristics), which makes it essential to reduce the total number of rows. For example, pictures may contain thousands of pixels, all those pixels are not important for the analysis. Or a large number of measurements or experiments can be applied to every single chip while testing microchips within the manufacturing process, majority of which produce redundant data. In such scenarios, "dimensionality reduction" algorithms are leveraged to manage the data set.

Principal Component Analysis

"Principal Component Analysis" or (PCA) is the most common "dimension reduction technique," which decreases the size of the "feature space" by discovering new vectors that are capable of maximizing the linear variety of the data. When the linear correlations of the data are powerful, PCA can dramatically decrease the data dimension without losing too much information. PCA is one of the fundamental algorithms of machine learning. It enables you to decrease the data dimension, losing as little information as possible. It is used in many fields such as object recognition, vision of computers, compression of information, etc. The calculation of the main parts is limited to the calculation of the initial data's own vectors and covariance matrix values or to the data matrix's unique decomposition. Through one we can convey several indications, merge, so to speak, and operate with a simpler model already. Of course, most probably, data loss will not be avoided, but the PCA technique will assist us to minimize any losses.

t-Stochastic Neighbor Embedding (t-SNE)

Another common technique is "t-Stochastic Neighbor Embedding (t-SNE)," which results in decrease of non-linear dimensionality. This technique is primarily used for data visualization, with potential use for machine learning functions such as space reduction and clustering.

The next plot demonstrates "MNIST database" analysis of handwritten digits. "MNIST" includes a large number of digit pictures from 0 to 9, used by scientists to test "clustering" and "classification" algorithms. Individual row of the data set represents "vectorized version" of the original picture (size 28x28 = 784 pixels) and a label (0, 1, 2 and so on) for each picture. Note that the dimensionality is therefore reduced from 784 pixels to 2-D in the plot below. Two-dimensional projecting enables visualization of the initial high-dimensional data set.

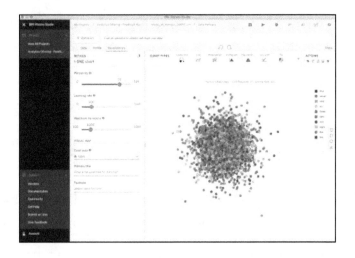

5. Ensemble Methods

Think that you have chosen to construct a car because you are not pleased with the variety of cars available in the market and online. You may start by discovering the best option for every component that you need. The resulting car will outshine all the other alternatives with the assembly of all these excellent components.

"Ensemble methods" use the same concept of mixing several predictive models (controlled machine learning) to obtain results of greater quality than any of the models can generate on their own. The "Random Forest" algorithms, for instance, is an "ensemble method" that collates various trained "Decision Trees" with different data set samples. Consequently, the quality of predictions generated by "Random Forest" method is better than the quality of the estimated predictions generated by only one "Decision Tree."

Think of "ensemble methods" as an approach for reducing a single machine learning model's variance and bias. This is essential because under certain circumstances, any specified model may be accurate but completely incorrect under other circumstances. The relative accuracy could be overturned with another model. The quality of the predictions is balanced by merging the two models.

6. Transfer Learning

Imagine you are a data scientist focusing on the clothing industry. You have been training a high-quality learning model for months to be able to classify pictures of "women's tops" as tops, tank tops and blouses. You have been tasked to create a comparable model for classification of pants pictures such as jeans, trousers and chinos. With the use of "Transfer Learning" method, the understanding incorporated into the first model be seamlessly transferred and applied to the second model.

Transfer Learning pertains to the re-use and adaptation of portion of a previously trained neural network to a fresh but comparable assignment. Specifically, once a neural network has been successfully trained for a particular task, a proportion of the trained layers can be easily transferred and combined with new layers which are then trained on pertinent data for the new task. This new "neural network" can learn and adapt rapidly to the new assignment by incorporating a few layers.

The primary benefit of transferring learning is decrease in the volume of data required to train the neural network resulting in cost savings for development of "deep learning algorithms." Not to forget how hard it can be to even procure sufficient amount of labeled data to train the model.

Suppose in this example, you are using a neural network with 20 hidden layers for the "women's top" model. You understand after running a few tests that 16 of the women's top model layers can be transferred and combined them with new set of data to train on pants pictures. Therefore, the new pants model will have 17 concealed layers. The input and output of both the tasks are distinct, but the reusable layers are capable of summarizing the data appropriate to both, e.g. clothing, zippers, and shape of the garment.

Transfer learning is getting increasingly popular, so much so that for basic "deep learning tasks" such as picture and text classification, a variety of high quality pre-trained models are already available in the market.

7. Natural Language Processing

A majority of the knowledge and information pertaining to our world is in some type of human language. Once deemed as impossible to achieve, today computers are capable of reading large volumes of books and blogs within minutes. Although, computers are still unable to fully comprehend "human text," but they can be trained to perform specific tasks. Mobile devices, for instance, can be trained to auto-complete text messages or fix spelling mistakes. Machines have been trained enough to hold straightforward conversations like humans.

"Natural Language Processing" (NLP) is not exactly a method of ML, instead it is a commonly used technique to produce texts for machine learning. Consider multitude of formats of tons of text files (words, internet blogs etc). Most of these text files are usually flooded with typing errors, grammatically incorrect characters and phrases that need to be filtered out. The most popular text processing model available in the market today is "NLTK (Natural Language ToolKit)," developed by "Stanford University" researchers.

The easiest approach to map texts into numerical representations is calculation of the frequency of each word contained in every text document. For example, an integer matrix where individual rows represent one text document and every column represents single word. This word frequency representation matrix is frequently referred to as the "Term Frequency Matrix" (TFM). From there, individual matrix entries can be separated by a weight of how essential every single term is within the whole stack of papers. This form of matrix representation of a text document is called as "Term Frequency Inverse Document Frequency" (TFIDF), which usually yields better performance for machine learning tasks.

8. Word Embedding

"Term Frequency Matrix" and "Term Frequency Inverse Document Frequency" are numerical representations of text papers which only take into account frequency and weighted frequencies to represent text files. On the other hand, "Word Embedding" in a document is capable of capturing the actual context of a word. Embedding can quantify the similarity between phrases within the context of the word, which subsequently allows execution of arithmetic operations with words.

"Word2Vec" is a neural network-based technique that can map phrases to a numerical vector in a corpus. These vectors are then used to discover synonyms, do arithmetic with words or phrases, or to represent text files. Let's suppose, for instance, a large enough body of text files was used to estimate word embedding. Suppose the words "king, queen, man and female" are found in the corpus and vector ("word") is the number vector representing the word "word." We can conduct arithmetic procedure with numbers to estimate vector('woman'):

vector('king') + vector('woman') — vector('man') ~ vector('queen')

Word depictions enable similarities to be found between phrases by calculating the "cosine similarity" between the vector representation of the two words. The "cosine similarity" gives a measure of the angle between two vectors.

We use machine learning techniques to calculate word embedding, but this is often a preliminary step in implementing a machine learning algorithm on top of the word embedding method. For example, the "Twitter" user database containing large volume of "tweets" can be leveraged to understand which of these customers purchased a house recently. We can merge "Word2Vec" with a logistic regression to generate predictions on the likelihood of a new "Twitter" user purchasing a home.

9. Decision Trees

To refresh your memory; a machine learning decision tree can be defined as "a tree like graphical representation of the decision-making process, by taking into consideration all the conditions or factors that can influence the decision and the consequences of those decisions." Decision trees are considered one of the simplest "supervised machine learning algorithms," with three main elements: "branch nodes" representing conditions of the data set, "edges" representing ongoing decision process and "leaf nodes" representing end of the decision.

The two types of decision trees are: "Classification tree" that is used to classify Data on the basis of the existing data available in the system; "Regression tree" which is used to make forecast for predictions for future events on the basis of the existing data in the system. Both of these trees are heavily used in machine learning algorithms. A widely used terminology for decision trees is "Classification and Regression trees" or "CART."

Let's look at how you can build a simple decision tree based on a real-life example.

Step 1: Identify what decision needs to be made, which will serve as a "root node" for the decision tree. For this example, decision needs to be made on "What would you like to do over the weekend?" Unlike real trees, decision tree has its roots on top instead of the bottom.

Step 2: Identify conditions or influencing factors for your decision which will serve as "branch nodes" for the decision tree. For this example, conditions could include "would you like to spend the weekend alone or with your friends?" and "how is the weather going to be?"

Step 3: As you answer the conditional questions, you may run into additional conditions that you might have ignored. You will now continue to your final decision by processing all the conditional questions individually, these bifurcations will serve as "edges" of your decision tree.

Step 4: Once you have processed all of the permutations and combinations and eventually made your final decision, that final decision will serve as the "leaf node" of your decision tree. Unlike "branch nodes," there are no further bifurcations possible from a "leaf node."

Below is the graphical representation of your decision for the example above.

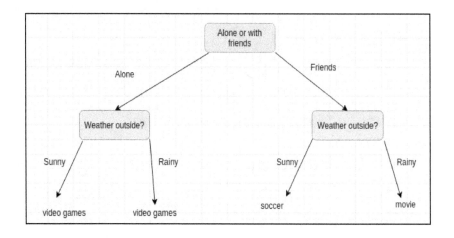

As you would expect from a decision tree, you have obtained a "model representing a set of sequential and hierarchical decisions that ultimately lead to some final decision." This example is at a very high-level to help you develop an understanding of the concept of decision trees. The data science and machine learning decision trees are much more complicated and bigger with hundreds and thousands of branch nodes and edges.

The best tool on the market to visualize and understand decision trees is "Scikit Learn." Machine learning decisions tree models can be developed using two steps: "Induction" and "Pruning."

Induction

In this step, the decision trees are actually developed by selecting and modeling all of the sequential and hierarchical decision boundaries on the basis of existing data set. For your ease of understanding, here are 4 high level steps required to develop the tree:

1. Gather, classify and label the training data set with "feature variables" and "classification or regression output."

2. Identify the best and most cost-effective feature within the training data set that will be used as the point for bifurcating the data.

3. Based on the possible values of the selected "best feature," create subsets of data by bifurcating the data set. These bifurcations will define the "branch nodes" of the decision tree, where in each node serves as a point of bifurcation based on specific features from the data set.

4. Iteratively develop new tree nodes with the use of data subsets gathered from the step 3. These bifurcations will continue until an optimal point is reached, where maximum accuracy is achieved while minimizing the number of bifurcations or nodes.

Pruning

The inherent purpose of decision trees is to support training and self learning of the system, which often requires over loading of all possible conditions and influencing factors that might affect the final result. To overcome the challenge of setting the correct output for least number of instances per node, developers make a "safe bet" by settling for that "least number" as rather small. This results in a high number of bifurcations on necessary, making for a very complex and large decision tree. This is where "tree pruning" comes into the picture. The verb "prune" literally means "to reduce especially by eliminating superfluous matter." This is the same kind of concept taken from real life tree pruning and applied to the data science and machine learning decision tree pruning process.

The process of pruning effectively reduces the overall complexity of the decision tree by "transforming and compressing strict and rigid decision boundaries into generalized and smooth boundaries." The number of bifurcations in the decision trees determine the overall complexity of the tree. The easiest and widely used pruning method is reviewing individual branch nodes and evaluating the effect of its removal on the cost function of the decision tree. If the cost function has little to no effect of the removal, then the branch node under review can be easily removed or "pruned."

10. Apriori machine learning algorithm

"Apriori algorithm" is another unsupervised ML algorithm that can produce rules of association from a specified set of data. "Association rule" simply means if an item X exists then the item Y has a predefined probability of existence. Most rules of association are produced in the format of "IF-THEN" statements. For instance, "IF" someone purchases an iPhone, "THEN" they have most likely purchased an iPhone case as well. The Apriori algorithm is able to draw these findings by initially observing the number of individuals who purchased an iPhone case while making an iPhone purchase and generating a ratio obtained by dividing the number individuals who bought a new iPhone (1000) with individuals who also bought an iPhone case (800) with their new iPhones.

The fundamental principles of Apriori ML Algorithm are:

- If a set of events have high frequency of occurrence, then all subsets of that event set will also have high frequency of occurrence.
- If a set of events occur occasionally, then all supersets of the event set of will occur occasionally as well.

Apriori algorithm has wide applicability in following areas:

"Detecting Adverse Drug Reactions"

"Apriori algorithm" is used to analyze healthcare data such as the drugs administered to the patient, characteristics of each patient, harmful side effects experienced by the patient, the original diagnosis, among others. This analysis generates rules of association that provide insight on the characteristic of the patient and the administered drug that potentially contributed to adverse side effects of the drug.

"Market Basket Analysis"

Some of the leading online e-commerce businesses including "Amazon," use Apriori algorithm to gather insights on products that have high likelihood of being bought together and products that can have an upsell with product promotions and discount offers. For instance, Apriori could be used by a retailer to generate prediction such as: customers purchasing sugar and flour have high likelihood of purchasing eggs to bake cookies and cakes.

"Auto-Complete Applications"

The highly cherished auto-complete feature on "Google" is another common Apriori application. When the user starts typing in their keywords for a search, the search engine searches its database, for other related phrases that are usually typed in after a particular word.

11. Support vector machine learning algorithm

"Support Vector Machine" or (SVM) is a type of "supervised ML algorithm," used for "classification" or "regression," where the data set trains SVM on "classes" in order to be able to classify new inputs. This algorithm operates by classifying the data into various "classes" by discovering a line (hyper-plane) that divides the collection of training data into "classes." Due to availability of various linear hyper-planes, this algorithm attempts to maximize the distance between the different "classes" involved, which is called as "margin maximization." By identifying the line that maximizes the class distance, the likelihood of generalizing apparent to unseen data can be improved.

SVM's can be categorized into two as follows:

- "Linear SVM's" – The training data or classifiers can be divided by a hyper-plane.
- "Non-Linear SVM's" – Unlike linear SVMs, in "non-linear SVM's" the possibility to separate the training data with a hyper-plane is nonexistent. For example, the Face Detection training data consists of a group of facial images and another group of non-facial images. The training data is so complicated under such circumstances, that it is difficult to obtain a feature representation of every single vector. It is extremely complex to separate the facial data set linearly from the non-facial data set.

SVM is widely used by different economic organizations for stock market forecasting. For example, SVM is leveraged to compare relative stock performances of various stocks in the same industrial sector. The classifications generated by SVM, aids in the investment related decision-making process.

The Kernel Trick

The data collected in the real world is randomly distributed and making it too difficult to separate different classes linearly. However, if we can potentially figure out a way to map the data from 2-dimensional space to 3-dimensional space, as shown in the picture below, we will be able to discover a decision surface that obviously separates distinct classes.

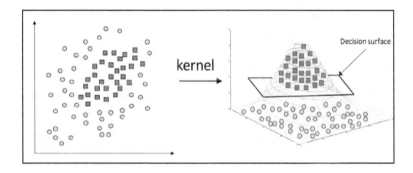

One approach to transform data like this is mapping all data points to a higher dimension (in this case, 3 dimensions), finding the limit, and making the classification. That works for limited number of dimensions but computations within given space becomes increasingly costly when there are a lot of dimensions to deal with. And so, the kernel trick comes to the rescue!

The "kernel trick" enables us to function in the original feature space without needing to calculate the data coordinates in a higher dimensional space. For example, the equation in the picture below has couple of 3-D data points as 'x' and 'y.'

$$\mathbf{x} = (x_1, x_2, x_3)^T$$
$$\mathbf{y} = (y_1, y_2, y_3)^T$$

Suppose we want to map 'x' and 'y' to 9-dimensional space. To get the final outcome, which would be just scalar, we have to do the calculations shown in the picture below. In this case, the computational complexity will be O(n2).

$$\phi(\mathbf{x}) = (x_1^2, x_1 x_2, x_1 x_3, x_2 x_1, x_2^2, x_2 x_3, x_3 x_1, x_3 x_2, x_3^2)^T$$
$$\phi(\mathbf{y}) = (y_1^2, y_1 y_2, y_1 y_3, y_2 y_1, y_2^2, y_2 y_3, y_3 y_1, y_3 y_2, y_3^2)^T$$

$$\phi(\mathbf{x})^T \phi(\mathbf{y}) = \sum_{i,j=1}^{3} x_i x_j y_i y_j$$

However, by using the "kernel function," which is denoted as 'k(x, y),' instead of doing the complex calculations in the 9-dimensional space, the same outcome can be achieved in the 3-dimensional space by calculating the "dot product" of 'x-transpose' and 'y.' In this case, the computational complexity will be O(n).

$$
\begin{aligned}
k(\mathbf{x}, \mathbf{y}) &= (\mathbf{x}^T \mathbf{y})^2 \\
&= (x_1 y_1 + x_2 y_2 + x_3 y_3)^2 \\
&= \sum_{i,j=1}^{3} x_i x_j y_i y_j
\end{aligned}
$$

In principle, the kernel trick is used to make the transformation of data into higher dimensions much more effective and less costly. The use of the kernel trick is not restricted to the SVM algorithm. The kernel trick can be used with any computations involving the "dot products (x, y)."

Chapter 3: Data Pre-processing and Creation of Training Data Set

Data Preprocessing is a "data mining technique, which is used to transform raw data into a comprehensible and effective format." Real-world data tends to lack certain behaviors or trends and is almost always incomplete, inconsistent and/or missing attribute values, flooded with errors or outliers. Preprocessing data is a proven way to solve such problems. This raw data or real data from the world can not be readily transmitted through a machine learning model. Therefore, before feeding real world data to a machine learning model, we need to clean and pre-process it.

Overview of Data Preprocessing

Data Cleaning

Many meaningless and missing sections can be found in the data. "Data cleaning" is performed in order to manage these inadequacies and constitutes handling data set that is missing values and consists of noisy data.

Missing Data

In this scenario, certain significant information in the data set is missing. It can be dealt with in different respects such as:

- **Ignoring the tuples:** This strategy is appropriate only if the dataset is big and numerous values within a tuple are lacking.
- **Fill the missing values:** This assignment can be done in different ways such as: manually completing the missing values using the mean attribute or the most relevant value.

Noisy Data

"Noisy data" is useless data that machines, or the machine learning model is unable to interpret. It can be generated as a result of defective data collection or mistakes in data entry, among others. It can be addressed using the methods below:

- **Binning Method:** This technique operates on sorted data to smoothen it out. The entire data set is split into equivalent size sections and then different techniques are used to finish the job.

Each section is fixed individually. To fix the entire data set in ago, all data points in a section can be substituted with its "mean" or most probable values.

- **Regression:** In this case, data can be smoothed out by fitting into a "regression function," which can be either "linear" (with one autonomous variable) or "multiple" (with various autonomous variables).

- **Clustering:** This technique is used to group comparable data points into a cluster. The outliers could be obtained with data points falling outside of the clusters or could not be detected.

Data Transformation

This technique is used to convert the data into format which is suitable for the data mining method. This includes the following ways:

- **Normalization:** This technique is used to scale data values within a defined range, for example, "-1.0 to 1.0" or "0.0 to 1.0."

- **Attribute Selection:** New data attributes can be generated from existing data set of characteristics, using this technique to assist in the data mining process.

- **Discretization:** This technique is used to "replace raw values of numerical attributes with interval or conceptual levels."

- **Generation of the concept of hierarchy:** This technique is used to transform lower level data attributes to higher level in the hierarchical set up. For example, you can convert the attribute "city" to "country."

Data Reduction

"Data mining" is a method used for analysis and extraction of insights from Big data. In such instances, analysis becomes more and more difficult to work with given the enormity of data. We use data reduction method to reduce the volume of data set to an optimal and manageable volume. With this method the cost of data storage and analysis can be significantly lowered while improving the effectiveness of the data storage. It can be dealt with in different respects such as:

- **Data Cube aggregation:** This technique is used to apply "aggregation operation" to data to effectively build data cubes.

- **Selection of attribute subset:** This technique is used to ensure that only necessary data attributes are used, and the not so relevant attributes can be discarded. To perform attribute selection, the "level of significance" and "p-value of the attribute" can be leveraged. The attribute with "p-value" higher than the "significance level" can be removed to obtain optimal volume of the data set.

- **Numerosity reduction:** This technique allows the data model to be stored instead of the whole data set or raw data collected from various input sources, for instance, "Regression Models."

- **Dimensionality reduction:** This technique uses encoding mechanisms to reduce the volume of the data set. If initial data set can be recovered after reconstruction from compressed data set, this reduction in dimensions of the data set is known as "lossless reduction," otherwise it is referred to as "loss reduction." The two efficient techniques of reducing data set "dimensionality" are: "Wavelet transforms" and "PCA (Principal Component Analysis)."

Steps of Data Pre-Processing

I – Import the Data Library

There is a wide variety of data libraries available that you can choose to meet your data requirements, such as:

"Pandas": Widely used for data visualization and data manipulation processes.

"NumPy": A basic package to perform scientific computations using Python.

"Matplotlib": A standard Python Library used by data scientists to create 2-D plots and graphs.

"Seaborn": Seaborn is derived from the "Matplotlib" library and an extremely popular visualization library.

For example, you can use the main libraries from "Pandas," "NumPy" and "time"; data visualization libraries from "Matplotlib" and "Seaborn"; and Scikit-Learn libraries for the data preprocessing techniques and algorithms.

To import the libraries mentioned above, use the code below:

For main libraries

"import pandas as pd

import numpy as np

import time"

For visualization libraries

"from matplotlib import pyplot as plt

import seaborn as sns

from mpl_toolkits.mplot3d import Axes3D

plt.style.use('ggplot')"

For Scikit-Learn libraries

"from sklearn.neighbors import KNeighborsClassifier

from sklearn.model_selection import train_test_split

from sklearn.preprocessing import normalize

from sklearn.metrics import

confusion_matrix,accuracy_score,precision_score,recall

_score,f1_score,matthews_corrcoef,classification_repor

t,roc_curve

from sklearn.externals import joblib

from sklearn.preprocessing import StandardScaler

from sklearn.decomposition import PCA"

II – Data exploration

To get some sense of the imported dataset in Pandas, use the code below:

```
"# Read the data in the CSV file using pandas
df = pd.read_csv(.'./input/creditcard.csv')
df.head()"
```

III – Check for missing values

It is essential to comprehend the concept of missing values to be able to effectively manage data. If the researcher does not handle the missing values correctly, they may end up drawing incorrect data inferences. Because of improper handling, the results produced will be different from those with missing values. You can apply any of the techniques below to deal with missing data values in your data set.

1. Ignore the data row

This is generally performed when the "class label" is missing or if multiple data attribute are missing in the row, assuming the data mining objective is classification. However, if the proportion of such rows with missing class labels is high, you will obviously get bad output.

For instance, database with enrolment data for the student (age, SAT score, address, etc.) containing a column with "Low," "Medium" and "High" to classify their achievement in college. Assuming the objective is to construct a model that predicts the college achievement of a student. Data rows that do not include the achievement column are not helpful to generate predictions regarding the success of the student, so they can be overlooked and deleted before the algorithm is executed.

2. Use a global constant to fill in for missing values

In this technique an appropriate and new global constant value is selected, such as "unknown," "N / A" or "minus infinity," which is then used to fill all the missing values. This technique is employed when the concerted effort to predict the missing value just doesn't make sense. Let's consider the student enrollment database example again, assume that some students lack information on the 'state of residence' attribute. It doesn't really make sense to fill it with some random state instead of using "N/A."

3. Use attribute mean

This technique is used to replace an attribute's missing values with the "mean or median value (if its discrete)," for specific attribute in the database. For instance, in a US family income database, if the average income of a family is X, that value can be used to replace missing values in the other family records.

4. Using attribute mean for all samples belonging to the same class

This technique is used to restrict the calculations to a particular class in order to obtain a value that is applicable to the row that we are searching for in lies of using the "mean (or medians)" of a particular attribute calculated by searching all the rows of the database. For example, if you have an automobile price database that classifies vehicles, among other things, into "Luxury" and "Low Budget." It is likely more precise to replace the missing price of a "luxury car" with the average price of all luxury vehicles instead of the value obtained after factoring in "low budget cars."

5. Use data mining algorithm to predict the most probable value

Data mining algorithms such as "Regression," "inference-based tools using Bayesian formalism," "decision trees," "clustering algorithms (K-Mean\Median etc.)" can be used to determine the probable value of the data attribute. For instance, "clustering algorithms" could be employed to produce cluster of rows that are then used to calculate the mean or median of the attribute as indicated earlier in the Technique 3. Another instance might be to use a "decision tree" to generate prediction for the most probable value of the missing attribute by taking into account all other attributes in the data set.

IV – Dealing with Categorical Data Values

Categorical attributes can only take on a restricted amount of feasible values, which are generally fixed. For instance, if a dataset is about user-related data, then characteristics such as 'nation,' 'gender,' 'age group,' etc. will constitute the data set. Alternatively, you will find attributes such as 'product type,' 'manufacturer,' 'vendor,' and so on if your data set pertains to a commodity or product.

In context of the data set, these are all categorical attributes. Typically, these attributes are stored as text values representing different characteristics of the observations. Gender is defined, for instance, as "male" or "female," and product type could be defined as "electronics," "apparel," "food" and so on.

There are three types of categorical data:

- **Nominal** – The types of attributes where categories are only labeled and have no order of succession are called "nominal features." For example, gender could be 'male' (M) or 'female' (F) and have no order of precedence.
- **Ordinal** – The types of attributes where categories are labeled with an order of precedence are called "ordinal features." For example, an economic status feature can contain three categories: "low," "medium" and "high," which have an inherent order associated with them.
- **Continuous** – The types of attributes where categories are numerical variables with infinite values ranging between two defined values are called "continuous features."

Challenges of Categorical Data

- Categorical attributes can contain multiple levels, called as "high cardinality" (e.g. states, towns or URLs), where most levels appear in relatively smaller number of instances.

- Various ML models are algebraic, such as "regression" and "SVM," which require numerical input. Categories have to be changed first to numbers in order to use these models, before the machine learning algorithm can be applied.

- While some machine learning packages or libraries are capable of automatically transforming the categorical data into numeric, depending on the default embedded technique, a variety of machine learning libraries don't support categorical data inputs.

- Categorical data for the computer does not translate the context or background, that people can readily associate with and comprehend. For instance, consider a function called "City" with different city names like "New York," "New Jersey," and "New Delhi." People know that "New York" is strongly linked to "New Jersey" being two neighboring states of America, while "New York" and "New Delhi" are very distinct. On the other hand, for the machine all three cities just denote three distinct levels of the same "City" function. Without specifying adequate context through data for the model, differentiating between extremely distinct levels will be difficult for it.

Encoding Categorical Data

Machine learning models are built on mathematical equations, so it is easy to comprehend that maintaining the categorical data in equations would cause issues since equations are primarily driven by numbers alone. To cross this hurdle, the categorical features can be encoded to numeric quantities.

The encoding techniques below will be described using example of an "airline carrier" column from a make-believe airline database, for ease of understanding. However, it is possible to extend the same techniques to any desired column.

1. Replacing the categorical values

This is a fundamental technique of replacing the categorical data values with required integers. The *"replace()"* function in Pandas, can be used for this technique. Depending on your business requirements, desired numbers can be easily assigned to the categorical values.

2. Encoding Labels

The technique of converting categorical values in a column to a number is called as "label encoding." Numerical labels always range from "0" to "n categories-1." Encoding a group of category to certain numerical value and then encoding all other categories to another numerical value can be done using the *"where()"* function in NumPy. For example, one could encode all the "US airline carriers" to value "1" and all other carriers can be given a value "0." You can perform similar label encoding using "Scikit-Learn's LabelEncoder."

Label encoding is fairly intuitive and simple and produce satisfactory performance from your learning algorithm. However, the algorithm is at a disadvantage and may misinterpret numerical values. For example, algorithm may confuse whether the "U.S. airline carrier" (encoded to 6) should be given 6 times more weight "U.S. airline carrier" (encoded to 1).

3. One-Hot encoding

To resolve the misinterpretation issue of the machine learning algorithm generated by the "label encoding" technique, each categorical data value can be transformed into a new column and that new column can be allocated a '1' or '0' (True/False) value, and is called as "one-hot encoding."

Of all the machine learning libraries in the market that offer "one-hot encoding," the easiest one is *"get_dummies()"* technique in "Pandas," which is appropriately titled given the fact that dummy/indicator data variables such as "1" or "0" are created. In its preprocessing module, Scikit-Learn also supports "one-hot encoding" in it's pre-processing module via "LabelBinarizer" and "OneHotEncoder" techniques.

While "one-hot encoding" addresses the issue of misinterpreted category weights, it gives rise to another issue. Creation of multiple new columns to solve this category weight problem for numerous categories can lead to a "curse of dimensionality." The logic behind "curse of dimensionality" is that some equations simply stop functioning correctly in high-dimensional spaces.

4. Binary encoding

This method initially encodes the categories as "ordinal," then converts these integers into binary string, and then divides digits of that binary code into distinct columns. Therefore, the data is encoded in only few dimensions unlike the "one-hot encoding" method.

There are several options to implement binary encoding in your machine learning model, but the easiest option is to install "category_encoders" library. This can be done using "pip install category_encoders" on cmd.

5. Backward difference encoding

This "backward difference encoding" method falls within the "contrast coding scheme" for categorical attributes. A "K" category or level characteristic typically enters a "regression" as a series of dummy "K-1" variables. This technique works by drawing a comparison between the "mean" of the dependent variable for a level with the "mean" of the dependent variable in the preceding stage. This kind of encoding is widely used for a "nominal" or an "ordinal "variable."

The code structure for this technique is quite the similar to any other technique in the "category_encoders" library, except the run command for this technique is "BackwardDifferenceEncoder."

6. Miscellaneous features

You may sometimes deal with categorical columns that indicate the range of values in observation points, for instance, an 'age' column can contain categories such as '0-20,' '20-40,' '40-60' etc. While there may be many methods to handle such attributes, the most popular ones are:

A. Dividing the categorical value ranges into two distinct columns, by first creating a dummy data frame with just one feature as "age" and then splitting the column on the delimiter "(-)" into two columns "start" and "end" using *"split()"* and *"lambda()"* functions .

B. Replacing the categorical value ranges with select measure like the mean value of the range, using function *"split_mean()."*

V – Splitting the Data Set into Training and Testing Data Subsets

The machine learning algorithms are required to learn from sample data set to be able to generate predictions from the input data set. In general, we divide the data set into a proportion of 70:30 or 80:20, which means that 70% of the data is used as the training subset and 30% of the data is used as the testing subset. However, this split ratio is adjusted according to the form and size of the data set.

It is almost impossible and futile to manually split the data set, while making sure the data set is divided randomly. The Scikit-Learn library offers us with a tool called the "Model Selection library," to assist with this task. There is a "class" in the Scikit-Learn library called *"train_test_split."* Using this, we can readily divide the data set into the "training" and "testing" datasets in desired ratios. Some parameters to consider while using this tool are:

- **Test_size** - It helps in determining the size of the data to be divided as the testing data set, as a fraction of the total data set. For example, entering 0.3 as the "test_size" value, the data set will be divided at 30 percent as the test data set. If you specify this parameter, the next parameter may be ignored.
- **Train_size** – This parameter is only specified if the "test_size" has not been specified already. The

process works similar to the "test_size" function, except that the percentage of the data set specified is for the "training set."

- **Random_state** - An integer is entered here for the Scikit-Learn class, on the basis of which the "random number generator" will be activated during the data set split. Alternatively, an instance of "RandomState" class can b entered that will then generate random numbers. If you don't enter either of the functions, the default will be activated which leverages the "RandomState" instance used by "np.random."

For example, the data set in the picture below can be split into two subsets: 'X' subset for the "independent features" and 'Y' subset for the "dependent variables" and also happens to be the last column of the data set.

Country	Age	Salary	Purchased
France	44	72000	No
Spain	27	48000	Yes
Germany	30	54000	No
Spain	38	61000	No
Germany	40	nan	Yes
France	35	58000	Yes
Spain	nan	52000	No
France	48	79000	Yes
Germany	50	83000	No
France	37	67000	Yes

Now we can use the code belwo to split the "x" data set into two subsets: "xTrain" and "xTest" and likewise, split the "y" data set into two subsets "yTrain" and "yTest."

"from sklearn.model_selection import train_test_split xTrain, xTest, yTrain, yTest = train_test_split(x, y, test_size = 0.2, random_state = 0)"

According to the code above, the test data set size will be 0.2 or 20% of the entire data set and the remaining 80% of the data set will be used as training data set.

Building Data Pipeline for Machine Learning

Computer programmers will typically "define a pipeline for data as it flows through their machine learning model." Every stage of the pipeline utilizes the data generated from the previous stage once it has processed the data as needed. The word "pipeline" can be a little misleading as it indicates a unidirectional flow of data, when in reality the machine learning pipelines are "cyclical and iterative," as each stage would be repeated in order to eventually produce an effective algorithm.

While looking to develop a machine learning model, programmers work in select development environments geared for "Statistics" and 'Machine Learning" such as Python and R among others. These environments enable training and testing of the models, using a single "sandboxed" environment, while writing reasonably fewer lines of code. This is excellent for the development of interactive prototypes that can be quickly launched in the market, instead of developing production systems with low latency.

The primary goal of developing a machine learning pipeline is to construct a model with features listed below:

- Should allow for reduction of system latency.
- Integration but loose coupling with other components of the model, such as data storage systems, reporting functionalities and "Graphical User Interface (GUI)."
- Should allow for horizontal as well as vertical scalability.
- Should be driven by messages, meaning the model should be able to communicate through the

transfer of "asynchronous, non-blocking messages."

- Ability to generate effective calculations for management of the data set.
- Should be resilient to system errors and be able to recover with minimal to no supervision, known as breakdown management.
- Should be able to support "batch processing" as well as "real-time" processing of the input data.

Conventionally, data pipelines require "overnight batch processing," which mean gathering the data, transmitting it with an "enterprise message bus" and then processing it to generate pre-calculated outcomes and guidelines for future transactions. While this model has proven to work in certain industrial sectors, in others, and particularly when it comes to machine learning models, "batch processing" doesn't meet the challenge.

The picture below demonstrates a machine learning data pipeline as applied to a real-time business problem in which attributes and projections are dependent on time taken to generate the results. For instance, product recommendation systems used by Amazon, system to estimate time of arrival used by Lyft, system to recommend potential new links used by LinkedIn, search engines used by Airbnb, among others.

The swim lane diagram above consists of two explicitly specified components:

1. "Online Model Analytics": In the top swim lane of the picture, the elements of the application required for operation are depicted. It shows where the model is used to make decisions in real-time.

2. "Offline Data Discovery": The bottom swim lane shows the learning element of the model, which is used to analyze historical data and generate the machine learning model using the "batch processing" method.

There are 8 fundamental stages in creation of a data pipeline, which are shown in the picture below and explained in detail here:

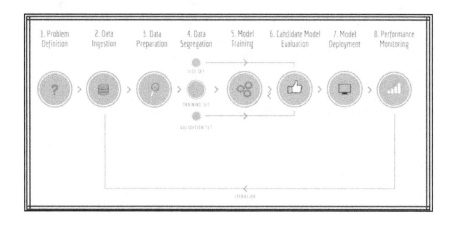

1. Problem Definition

In this stage, the business problem that needs to be resolved using a machine learning model will be identified and documented with all pertinent details.

2. Data Ingestion

The first stage of any machine learning workflow is to channel input data into a database server. The most important thing thing to remember is that the data is ingested raw and with no modification to enable us to have an invariable record of the original dataset. Data may be supplied from a variety of sources which can be acquired either through request or transmitted from other systems.

"NoSQL document databases" are best suited to store huge amount of defined and labeled as well as unorganized raw data, that are quickly evolving as they do not need to adhere to a predefined scheme. It even provides a "distributed, scalable and replicated data storage."

"Offline"

Data will flow in the "offline" layer to the raw data storage through an "Ingestion Service," which is a "composite orchestration service that is capable of encapsulating the data sourcing and persistence." A repository model is used internally to communicate with a data service that will interact with the data storage in exchange. When you save the data in the database, a unique batch Id will be given to the dataset, which allows for effective query of the data as well as end-to-end tracking and monitoring of the data.

To be computationally efficient, the ingestion of the data is distributed into two folds.

- The first one is a specific pipeline for every dataset so that each of the datasets can be processed individually and simultaneously.

- The second aspect is that within each pipeline data can be divided to make the best of a variety of server cores, processors and perhaps even the entire server.

Distributing the prepping of data across several vertical and horizontal pipelines, will reduce the total time required to perform the tasks.

The "ingestion service" would run at regular intervals on the basis of a predefined schedule (one or more times a day) or upon encountering a trigger. A subject will decouple producers (data source) from processors, which would be the data pipeline for this example, so when the source data is collected, the "producer system" will send a notification to the "broker" and subsequently the "embedded notification service" will respond by inducing ingestion of the data. The "notification service" would also inform the "broker" that the processing of the original dataset was completed with success and now the dataset is being stored in the database.

"Online"

The "Online Ingestion Service" makes up the entrance to the "streaming architecture" of the online layer, as it would decouple and manage the data flow from the source to the processing and storage components by offering consistent, high performance, low latency functionalities. It also works as an enterprise level "Data Bus." Data would be stored on a long-term "Raw Data Storage," which also serves as a mediating layer to the subsequent online streaming service for further processing in real-time. For instance, such techniques that are utilized in this case may be "Apache Kafka (pub / sub messaging system)" and "Apache Flume (data collection to long-term database)." A variety of other similar techniques are available and can be selectively applied based on the technology stack of the business.

3. Data Preparation

After the information has been ingested, a centralized pipeline would be produced that can evaluate the condition of the data, meaning it would search for format variations, outliers, patterns, inaccurate, incomplete or distorted information and correct any abnormalities through the process. The "feature engineering process" is also included in this stage. The 3 primary characters of a feature pipeline as depicted in the picture below are: "extraction, transformation and selection."

Phase	Input	Output
Extract	Raw data	Feature
Transform	Feature	Feature
Select	List<Feature>	List<Feature>

Since this tends to be the most complicated component of any machine learning project, it is essential to introduce appropriate design patterns. In context of coding it implies the use of a factory technique to produce features on the basis of certain shared abstract function behavior and a strategy pattern for selecting the correct features at the time of execution can be considered a logical approach. It is important to take into consideration the composition and re-usability of the pipeline while structuring the "feature extractors" and the "transformers."

The selection of functionalities could be attributed to the caller or could be automated. For instance, a "chi-square statistical test" can be applied to classify the impact of each functionality on the concept label, while discarding the low impact features before starting to train the model. To accomplish this, a number of "selector APIs" can be identified. In any case, a unique Id must be allocated to each feature set so as to make sure that the features used as model inputs and for impact scoring are consistent. Overall, it is necessary to assemble a data preparation pipeline into a set of unalterable transformations, which could be readily combined. Now the importance of "testing and high code coverage" will become a critical factor in the success of the model.

4. Data Segregation

The primary goal of the machine learning model is development of a high accuracy model on the basis of the quality of its forecasts and predictions for information derived from the new input data, which was not part of the training dataset. Therefore, available labeled dataset will be utilize as a "proxy" for future unknown input data by dividing the data into training and testing datasets. Many approaches are available to split the dataset and some of the most widely used techniques are:

- Using either the default or customized ratio to sequentially divide the dataset into two subsets in order to ensure that there is no overlap in the sequence in which the data appears from the source. For example, you could select the first 75% of data to train the model and the consequent 25% of data to test the accuracy of the model.

- Splitting the dataset into training and testing subset using a default or custom ratio with random seed. For example, you could choose a random 75% of the dataset to train the model and the remaining 25% of the random dataset to test the model.

- Using either of these techniques ("sequential vs. random") and then also mixing the data within each data subset.

- Using a customized injected approach for splitting the data when extensive control over segregation of the data is required.

Technically the data segregation stage is not considered as an independent machine learning pipeline, however an "API" or tool has to be provided to support this stage. In order to return the required datasets, the next 2 stages ("model training" and "model assessment") must be able to call this "API." As far as organization of the code is concerned, a "strategy pattern" is required so that the "caller service" can select the appropriate algorithm during execution and the capability to inject the percentage or random seed is obviously required. The "API" must also be prepared to return the information with or without labels, to train and test the model respectively. A warning can be created and passed along with the dataset to secure the "caller service" from defining parameters that could trigger uneven distribution of the data.

5. Model Training

The model pipelines are always "offline," and its schedule will vary from a matter of few hours to just one run per day, based entirely on the complexity of the application. The training can also be initiated by time and event, and not just by the system schedulers.

It includes a number of libraries of machine learning algorithms such as "linear regression, ARIMA, k-means, decision trees" and many more, which are designed to make provisions for rapid production of new model types as well as making the models interchangeable. Containment is also important for the integration of "third-Party APIs" using the "facade pattern" (at this stage the "Python Jupyter notebook" can also be called).

You have several choices for "parallelization":

- A specialized pipeline for individual models tends to be the easiest method, which means all the models can be operated at the same time.
- Another approach would be to duplicate the training dataset, i.e. the dataset can be divided, and each data set will contain a replica of the model. This approach is favored for the models that require all fields of an instance for performing the computations, for example, "LDA," 'MF."
- Another approach can be to parallelize the entire model, meaning the model can be separated and every partition can be responsible for the maintenance of a fraction of the variables. This approach is best suited for linear machine learning models like "Linear Regression," "Support Vector Machine."
- Lastly, a hybrid strategy could also be utilized by leveraging a combination of one or more of the approaches mentioned above.

It is important to implement train the model while taking error tolerance into consideration. The data check points and failures on training partitions must also be taken into account, for example, if every partition fails owing to some transient problem like timeout, then every partition could be trained again.

6. Candidate Model Evaluation

The model evaluation stage is also always "offline." By drawing comparison of the predictions generated with the testing dataset with the actual data values using several key performance indicators and metrics, the "predictive performance" of a model can be measured. To generate prediction on future input data, the "best" model from the testing subset will be preferred. An evaluator library consisting of a number of evaluators, can be designed to generate accuracy metrics such as "ROC curve" or "PR curve," which can also be stored in a data storage against the model. Once more, the same techniques are applied to make it possible to flexibly combine and switch between evaluators.

The "Model Evaluation Service" will request the testing dataset from the "Data Segregation API" to orchestrate the training and testing of the model. Moreover, the corresponding evaluators will be applied for the model originating from the "Model Candidate repository." The findings of the test will be returned to and saved in the repository. In order to develop the final machine learning model, an incremental procedure, hyper-parameter optimization as well as regularization methods would be used. The best model would be deemed as deployable to the production environment and eventually released in the market. The deployment information will be published by the "notification service."

7. Model Deployment

The machine learning model with highest performance will be marked for deployment for "offline (asynchronous)" and "online (synchronous)" prediction generation. It is recommended to deploy multiple models at the same time to ensure the transfer from obsolete to the current model is made smoothly, this implies that the services must continue to respond to forecast requirements without any lapse, while the new model is being deployed.

Historically, the biggest issue concerning deployment has been pertaining to the coding language required to operate the models have not been the same as the coding language used to build them. It is difficult to operationalize a "Python or R" based model in production using languages such as "C++, C #or Java." This also leads to major reduction in the performance in terms of speed and accuracy, of the model being deployed. This problem can be dealt with in a few respects as listed below:

- Implementing new language for rewriting the code, for example, "Python to C# translate."
- Creating customized "DSL (Domain Specific Language)" to define the model.
- Creating a "micro-service" that is accessible through "RESTful APIs."
- Implementing an "API first" approach through the course of deployment.
- Creating containers to store the code independently.
- Adding serial numbers to the model and loading them to a "in-memory key-value storage."

In practice the deployment activities required to implement an actual model are automated through the use of "continuous delivery implementation," which ensures the packaging of the necessary files, validation of the model via a robust test suite as well as the final deployment into a running container. An automated building pipeline can be used to execute the tests, which makes sure that the short, self-containing and stateless unit tests are conducted first. When the model has passed these tests, its quality will be evaluated in larger integrations and by executing regression tests. If both the test phases have been cleared, the model is deemed ready for deployment in the production environment.

8. Model Scoring

The terms "Model Scoring" and "Model Serving" are being used synonymously throughout the industry. Model Scoring" can be defined as "the process of generating new values with a given model and new input data." Instead of the term "prediction," a generic term "score" is being used to account for the distinct values it may lead to, as listed below:

- List of product recommendations.
- Numerical values, for the "time series models" as well as "regression models."

- A "probability value" that indicates the probability that a new input can be added to a category that already exists in the model.
- An alphabetical value indicating the name of a category that most closely resembles the new input data.
- A "predicted class or outcome" can also be listed as a model score particularly for "classification models."

After the models have been deployed they can be utilized to score on the basis of the feature data supplied by the prior pipelines or provided directly by a "client service." It is critical that the models generate predictions with same accuracy and high performance, in both the online and the offline mode.

"Offline"

The "scoring service" would be optimized in the offline layer for a big volume of data to achieve high performance and generate "fire and forget" predictions. A model is able to send an "asynchronous request" to initiate its scoring, however, it must wait for the batch scoring process to be completed and gain access to the batch scoring results before the scoring can be started. The "scoring service" will prepare the data, produce the features as well as retrieve additional features from the "Feature Data Store." The results of the scoring will be stored in the "Score Data Store," once the scoring has been completed. The "broker" will be informed of the completion of the scoring by receiving a notification from the service. This event is detected by the model, which will then proceed to collect the scoring results.

"Online"

In the "online" mode, a "client" will send a request to the "Online Scoring Service." The client can potentially request to invoke a specific version of the model, to allow the "Model Router" to inspect the request and subsequently transfer the request to the corresponding model.   According to request and in the same way as the offline layer, the "client service" will also prepare the data, produces the features and if needed, fetch additional functions from the "Feature Data Store." When the scoring has been done, the scores will be stored in the "Score Data Store" and then returned via the network to the "client service."

Totally dependent on the use case, results may be supplied asynchronously to the "client," which means the scored will be reported independent of the request using one of the two methods below:

- Push: After the scores have been obtained, they will be pushed to the "client" in the form of a "notification."
- Poll: After the scores have been produced, they will be saved in a "low read-latency database" and the client will poll the database at regular interval to fetch any existing predictions.

There are couple of techniques listed below, that can be used to reduce the time taken by the system to deliver the scores, once the request has been received:

- The input features can be saved in a "low-read latency in-memory data store."
- The predictions that have already been computed through an "offline batch-scoring" task can be cached for convenient access as dictated by the use-case, since "offline predictions" may lose their relevance.

9. Performance Monitoring

A very well-defined "performance monitoring solution" is necessary for every machine learning model. For the "model serving clients," some of the data points that you may want to observe include:

- "Model Identifier"
- "Deployment date and time"
- The "number of times" the model was served.
- The "average, min and max" of the time it took to serve the model.
- The "distribution of the features" that were utilized.
- The difference between the "predicted or expected results" and the "actual or observed results."

Throughout the model scoring process, this metadata can be computed and subsequently used to monitor the model performance.

Another "offline pipeline" is the "Performance Monitoring Service," which will be notified whenever a new prediction has been served and then proceed to evaluate the performance while persisting the scoring result and raising any pertinent notifications. The assessment will be carried out by drawing a comparison between the scoring results to the output created by the training set of the data pipeline. To implement fundamental performance monitoring of the model, a variety of methods can be used. Some of the widely used methods include "logging analytics" such as "Kibana," "Grafana" and "Splunk."

A low performing model that is not able to generate predictions at high speed will trigger the scoring results to be produced by the preceding model, to maintain the resiliency of the machine learning solution. A strategy of being incorrect rather than being late is applied, which implies that if the model requires extended period to time for computing a specific feature then it will be replaced by a preceding model in lieu of blocking the prediction. Furthermore, the scoring results will be connected to the actual results as they are accessible. This implies continuously measuring the precision of the model and at the same time any sign of deterioration in the speed of the execution can be handled by returning to the preceding model. In order to connect the distinct versions together, a "chain of responsibility pattern" could be utilized. The monitoring of the performance of the models is an on-going method, considering that a simple prediction modification can cause a model structure to be reorganized. Remember the advantages of machine learning model are defined by its ability to generate predictions and forecasts with high accuracy and speed to contribute to the success of the company.

Chapter 4: Scikit-Learn

Machine learning libraries are sensitive routines and functions that are written in any given language. Software developers require a robust set of libraries to perform complex tasks without needing to rewrite multiple lines of code. Machine learning is largely based upon mathematical optimization, probability and statistics.

Python is the language of choice in the field of machine learning credited to consistent development time and flexibility. It is well suited to develop sophisticated models and production engines that can be directly plugged into production systems. One of its greatest assets being an extensive set of libraries that can help researchers who are less equipped with developer knowledge to easily execute machine learning.

"Scikit-Learn" has evolved as the gold standard for machine learning using Python, offering a wide variety of "supervised" and "unsupervised" ML algorithms. It is touted as one of the most user friendly and cleanest machine learning libraries to date. For example, decision trees, clustering, linear and logistics regressions and K-means. Scikit-learn uses couple of basic Python libraries: NumPy and SciPy and adds a set of algorithms for data mining tasks including classification, regression and clustering. It is also capable of implementing tasks like feature selection, transforming data and ensemble methods in only a few lines.

In 2007, David Cournapeau, developed the foundational code of "Scikit-Learn" as part of a "Summer of code" project for "Google." Scikit-learn has become one of Python's most famous open source machine learning libraries since its launch in 2007. But it wasn't until 2010 that Scikit-Learn was released for public use. Scikit-Learn is an open sourced and BSD licensed, data mining and data analysis tool used to develop supervise and unsupervised machine learning algorithms build on Python. Scikit-learn offers various ML algorithms such as "classification," "regression," "dimensionality reduction," and "clustering." It also offers modules for feature extraction, data processing, and model evaluation.

Designed as an extension to the "SciPy" library, Scikit-Learn is based on "NumPy" and "matplotlib," the most popular Python libraries. NumPy expands Python to support efficient operations on big arrays and multidimensional matrices. Matplotlib offers visualization tools and science computing modules are provided by SciPy. For scholarly studies, Scikit-Learn is popular because it has a well-documented, easy-to-use and flexible API. Developers are able to utilize Scikit-Learn for their experiments with various algorithms by only altering a few lines of the code. Scikit-Learn also provides a variety of training datasets, enabling developers to focus on algorithms instead of data collection and cleaning. Many of the algorithms of Scikit-Learn are quick and scalable to all but huge datasets. Scikit-learn is known for its reliability and automated tests are available for much of the library. **Scikit-learn is extremely popular with beginners in machine learning to start implementing simple algorithms.**

Prerequisites for Application of Scikit-Learn Library

The Scikit-Learn library is based on the SciPy (Scientific Python), which needs to be installed before using SciKit-Learn. This stack involves the following:

NumPy (Base n-dimensional array package)

"NumPy" is the basic package with Python to perform scientific computations. It includes among other things: "a powerful N-dimensional array object; sophisticated (broadcasting) functions; tools for integrating C/C++ and Fortran code; useful linear algebra, Fourier transform, and random number capabilities." NumPy is widely reckoned as effective multi-dimensional container of generic data in addition to its apparent scientific uses. It is possible to define arbitrary data types. This enables NumPy to integrate with a broad variety of databases seamlessly and quickly. The primary objective of NumPy is the homogeneity of multidimensional array. It consists of an element table (generally numbers), all of which are of the same sort and are indicated by tuples of non-negative integers. The dimensions of NumPy are called "axes" and array class is called "ndarray."

Matplotlib (Comprehensive 2D/3D plotting)

"Matplotlib" is a 2-dimensional graphic generation library from Python that produces high quality numbers across a range of hardcopy formats and interactive environments. The "Python script," the "Python," "IPython shells," the "Jupyter notebook," the web app servers, and select user interface toolkits can be used with matplottib. Matplotlib attempts to further simplify easy tasks and make difficult tasks feasible. With only a few lines of code, you can produce tracks, histograms, scatter plots, bar graphs, error graphs, etc.

A MATLAB-like interface is provided for easy plotting of the Pyplot Module, especially when coupled with IPython. As a power user you can regulate the entire line styles, fonts properties and axis properties, through an object-oriented interface or through a collection of features similar to the one provided to MATLAB users.

SciPy (Fundamental library for scientific computing)

SciPy is a "collection of mathematical algorithms and convenience functions built on the NumPy extension of Python," capable of adding more impact to interactive Python sessions, by offering high-level data manipulation and visualization commands and courses for the user. An interactive Python session with SciPy becomes an environment that rival's data processing and system prototyping technologies including "MATLAB, IDL, Octave, R-Lab, and SciLab."

Another advantage of developing "SciPy" on Python, is the accessibility of a strong programming language in the development of advanced programs and specific apps. Scientific apps using SciPy benefit from developers around the globe developing extra modules in countless software landscape niches. Everything produced has been made accessible to the Python programmer, from database subroutines and classes as well as "parallel programming to web." These powerful tools are provided along with the "SciPy" mathematical libraries.

IPython (Enhanced interactive console)

"IPython (Interactive Python)" is an interface or command shell for interactive computing using a variety of programming languages. "IPython" was initially created exclusively for Python, which supports introspection, rich media, shell syntax, tab completion, and history. Some of the functionalities provided by IPython include: "interactive shells (terminal and Qt-based); browser-based notebook interface with code, text, math, inline plots and other media support; support for interactive data visualization and use of GUI tool kits; flexible interpreters that can be embedded to load into your own projects; tools for parallel computing."

SymPy (Symbolic mathematics)

Developed by Ondřej Čertík and Aaron Meurer, SymPy is "an open source Python library for symbolic computation." It offers algebra computing abilities to other apps, as a stand-alone app and/or as a library as well as live on the internet applications with "SymPy Live" or "SymPy Gamma." "SymPy" is easy to install and test, owing to the fact that it is completely developed in Python boasting limited dependencies. SymPy involves characteristics ranging from calculus, algebra, discrete mathematics, and quantum physics to fundamental symbolic arithmetic. The outcome of the computations can be formatted as "LaTeX" code. In combination with a straightforward, expandable code base in a widespread programming language, the ease of access provided by SymPy makes it a computer algebra system with comparatively low entry barrier.

Pandas (Data structures and analysis)

Pandas provide highly intuitive and user-friendly high-level data structures. Pandas has achieved popularity in the machine learning algorithm developer community, with built-in techniques for data aggregation, grouping and filtering as well as results of time series analysis. The Pandas library has two primary structures: one-dimensional "Series" and two-dimensional "Data Frames."

Seaborn (data visualization)

Seaborn is derived from the Matplotlib Library and an extremely popular visualization library. It is a high-level library that can generate specific kind of graph including heat map, time series and violin plots.

Installing Scikit-Learn

The latest version of Scikit-Learn can be found on "Scikit-Learn.org" and requires "Python (version >= 3.5); NumPy (version >= 1.11.0); SciPy (version >= 0.17.0); joblib (version >= 0.11)." The plotting capabilities or functions of Scikit-learn start with "plot_" and require "Matplotlib (version >= 1.5.1)." Certain Scikit-Learn examples may need additional applications: "Scikit-Image (version >= 0.12.3), Pandas (version >= 0.18.0)."

With prior installation of "NumPy" and "SciPy," the best method of installing Scikit-Learn is using "pip: pip install -U scikit-learn" or "conda: conda install scikit-learn."

One must make sure that "binary wheels" are utilized when using pip and that "NumPy" and "SciPy" have not been recompiled from source, which may occur with the use of specific OS and hardware settings (for example, "Linux on a Raspberry Pi"). Developing "NumPy" and "SciPy" from source tends to be complicated (particularly on Windows), therefore, they need to be setup carefully making sure optimized execution of linear algebra routines is achievable.

Application of Machine Learning Using Scikit-Learn Library

To understand how Scikit-Learn library is used in development of machine learning algorithm, let us use the "Sales_Win_Loss data set from IBM's Watson repository" containing data obtained from sales campaign of a wholesale supplier of automotive parts. We will build a machine learning model to predict which sales campaign will be a winner and which will incur loss.

The data set can be imported using Pandas and explored using Pandas techniques such as "head(), tail() and dtypes()." The plotting techniques from "Seaborn" will be used to visualize the data. To process the data Scikit-Learn's "preprocessing.LabelEncoder()" will be used and "train_test_split()" to divide the data set into training subset and testing subset.

To generate predictions from our data set, three different algorithms will be used namely, "Linear Support Vector Classification and K-nearest neighbors' classifier." To compare the performances of these algorithms Scikit-Learn library technique "accuracy_score" will be used. The performance score of the models can be visualized using Scikit-Learn and "Yellowbrick" visualization.

Importing the Data Set

To import the "Sales_Win_Loss data set from IBM's Watson repository," first step is importing the "Pandas" module using *"import pandas as pd."*

Then we leverage a variable url as *"https://community.watsonanalytics.com/wp content/uploads/2015/04/WA_Fn-UseC_-Sales-Win-Loss.csv"* to store the URL from which the data set will be downloaded.

Now, *"read_csv() as sales_data = pd.read_csv(url)"* technique will be used to read the above "csv or comma separated values" file, which is supplied by the Pandas module. The csv file will then be converted into a Pandas data framework, with the return variable as *"sales_data,"* where the framework will be stored.

For new 'Pandas' users, the *"pd.read csv()"* technique in the code mentioned above will generate a tabular data structure called "data framework," where an index for each row is contained in the first column, and the label / name for each column in the first row are the initial column names acquired from the data set. In the above code snippet, the "sales data" variable results in a table depicted in the picture below.

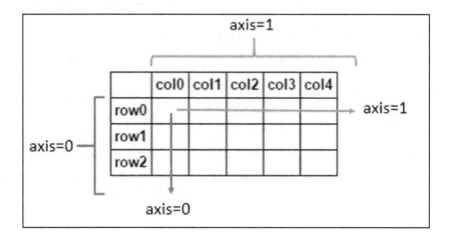

In the diagram above, the "row0, row1, row2" represent individual record index and the "col0, col1, col2" represent the names for individual columns or features of the data set.

With this step you have successfully stored a copy of the data set and transformed it into a "Pandas" framework!

Now, using the "head() as Sales_data.head()" technique the records from the data framework can be displayed as shown below to get a "feel" of the information contained in the data set.

	opportunity number	supplies subgroup	supplies group	region	route to market	elapsed days in sales stage	opportunity result
0	1641984	Exterior Accessories	Car Accessories	Northwest	Fields Sales	76	Won
1	1658010	Exterior Accessories	Car Accessories	Pacific	Reseller	63	Loss
2	1674737	Motorcycle Parts	Performance & Non-auto	Pacific	Reseller	24	Won
3	1675224	Shelters & RV	Performance & Non-auto	Midwest	Reseller	16	Loss

Data Exploration

Now that we have our own copy of the data set which has been transformed it into a "Pandas" data frame, we can quickly explore the data to understand what information can tell can be gathered from it and accordingly to plan a course of action.

In any ML project, data exploration tends to be a very critical phase. Even a fast data set exploration can offer us significant information that could be easily missed otherwise, and this information can propose significant questions that we can then attempt to answer using our project.

Some third-party Python libraries will be used here to assist us with the processing of the data, so that we can efficiently use this data with the powerful algorithms of Scikit-Learn. The same *"head()"* technique that we used to see the some initial records of the imported data set in the earlier section can be used here. As a matter of fact, *"(head)"* is effectively capable of doing much more than displaying data record and customize the "head()" technique to display only a selected records with commands like *"sales_data.head(n=2)."* This command will selectively display the first 2 records of the data set. At a quick glance it's obvious, that columns such as "Supplies Group" and "Region" contain string data, while columns such as "Opportunity Result," "Opportunity Number" etc. are comprised of integer values. It can also be seen that there are unique identifiers for each record in the' Opportunity Number' column.

Similarly, to display select records from the bottom of the table, the *"tail() as sales_data.tail()"* can be used.

To view the different data types available in the data set, the Pandas technique *"dtypes() as sales_data.dtypes"* can be used. With this information, the data columns available in the data framework can be listed with their respective data types. We can figure our, for example, that the column "Supplies Subgroup" is an "object" data type and that the column "Client Size By Revenue" is an "integer data type." So, we have an understanding of columns that either contain integer values or string data.

Data Visualization

At this point we are through with basic data exploration steps, so we will not attempt to build some appealing plots to portray the information visually and discover other concealed narratives from our data set.

Of all the available python libraries providing data visualization features; "Seaborn" is one of the best available options so we will be using the same. Make sure that python plots module provided by "Seaborn" has been installed on your system and ready to be used. Now follow the steps below generate desired plot for the data set:

Step 1 - Import the "Seaborn" module with command *"import seaborn as sns."*

Step 2 - Import the "Matplotlib" module with command *"import matplotlib.pyplot as plt."*

Step 3 - To set the "background colour" of the plot as white, use command *"sns.set(style="whitegrid,"* *color_codes=True)."*

Step 4 - To set the "plot size" for all plots, use command *"sns.set(rc={'figure.figsize':(11.7,8.27)})."*

Step 5 – To generate a "countplot," use command *"sns.countplot('Route To Market,'data=sales_data,hue = 'Opportunity Result')."*

Step 6 – To remove the top and bottom margins, use command *"sns.despine(offset=10, trim=True)."*

Step 7 – To display the plot, , use command *"plotplt.show()."*

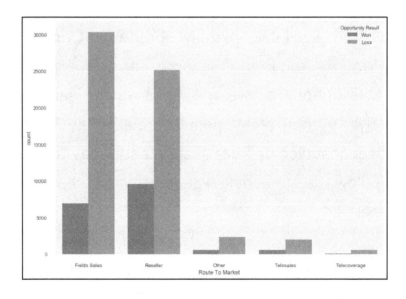

Quick recap - The "Seaborn" and "Matplotlib" modules were imported first. Then the *"set()"* technique was used to define the distinct characteristics for our plot, such as plot style and color. The background of the plot was defined to be white using the code snippet *"sns.set(style= "whitegrid," color codes= True)."* Then the plot size was define using command *"sns.set(rc={'figure.figsize':(11.7,8.27)})"* that define the size of the plot as "11.7px and 8.27px."

Next the command *"sns.countplot('Route To Market,'data= sales data, hue='Opportunity Result')"* was used to generate the plot. The "countplot()" technique enables creation of a count plot, which can expose multiple arguments to customize the count plot according to our requirements. As part of the first *"countplot()"* argument, the X-axis was defined as the column "Route To Market" from the data set. The next argument concerns the source of the data set, which would be "sales_data" data framework we imported earlier. The third argument is the color of the bar graphs that was defined as "blue" for the column labeled "won" and "green" for the column labeled "loss."

Data Pre-Processing

By now you should have a clear understanding of what information is available in the data set. From the data exploration step, we established that majority of the columns in our data set are "string data," but "Scikit-Learn" can only process numerical data. Fortunately, the Scikit-Learn library offers us many ways to convert string data into numerical data, for example, "LabelEncoder()" technique. To transform categorical labels from the data set such as "won" and "loss" into numerical values, we will use the "LabelEncoder()" technique.

Let's look at the pictures below to see what we are attempting to accomplish with the "LabelEncoder()" technique. The first image contains one column labeled "color" with three records namely, "Red," "Green" and "Blue." Using the "LabelEncoder()" technique, the record in the same "color" column can be converted to numerical values, as shown in second image.

	Color
0	Red
1	Green
2	Blue

	Color
0	1
1	2
2	3

Let's begin the real process of conversion now. Using the *"fit transform()"* technique given by *"LabelEncoder(),"* the labels in the categorical column like "Route To Market" can be encoded and converted to numerical labels comparable to those shown in the diagrams above. The function *"fit transform()"* requires input labels identified by the user and consequently returns encoded labels.

To know how the encoding is accomplished, let's go through an example quickly. The code instance below constitutes string data in form of a list of cities such as ["paris," "paris," "tokyo," "amsterdam"] that will be encoded into something comparable to "[2, 2, 1,3]."

Step 1 - To import the required module, use command *"from sklearn import preprocessing."*

Step 2 – To create the Label encoder object, use command *"le = preprocessing.LabelEncoder()."*

Step 3 – To convert the categorical columns into numerical values, use command:

"encoded_value = le.fit_transform(["paris," "paris," "tokyo," "amsterdam"])"

"print(encoded_value) [1 1 2 0]"

And there you have it! We just converted our string data labels into numerical values. The first step was importing the preprocessing module that offers the *"LabelEncoder()"* technique. Followed by development of an object representing the *"LabelEncoder()"* type. Then the *"fit_transform()"* function of the object was used to distinguish between distinct classes of the list ["paris," "paris," "tokyo," "amsterdam"] and output the encoded values of "[1 1 20]."

Did you observe that the *"LabelEncoder()"* technique assigned the numerical values to the classes in alphabetical order according to the initial letter of the classes, for example "(a)msterdam" was assigned code "0," "(p)aris" was assigned code "1" and "(t)okyo" was assigned code "2."

Creating Training and Test Subsets

To know the interactions between distinct characteristics and how these characteristics influence the target variable, a ML algorithm must be trained on a collection of information. We need to split the complete data set into two subsets to accomplish this. One subset will serve as the training data set, which will be used to train our algorithm to construct machine learning models. The other subset will serve as the test data set, which will be used to test the accuracy of the predictions generate by the machine learning model.

The first phase in this stage is separation of feature and target variables using the steps below:

Step 1 – To select data excluding select columns, use command *"select columns other than 'Opportunity Number,' 'Opportunity Result'cols = [col for col in sales_data.columns if col not in ['Opportunity Number,"Opportunity Result']]."*

Step 2 – To drop these select columns, use command *"dropping the 'Opportunity Number'and 'Opportunity Result' columns*
data = sales_data[cols]."

Step 3 – To assign the Opportunity Result column as "target," use command *"target = sales_data['Opportunity Result']*
data.head(n=2)."

The "Opportunity Number" column was removed since it just acts as a unique identifier for each record. The "Opportunity Result" contains the predictions we want to generate, so it becomes our "target" variable and can be removed from the data set for this phase. The first line of the above code will select all the columns except "Opportunity Number" and "Opportunity Result" in and assign these columns to a variable "cols." Then using the columns in the "cols" variable a new data framework was developed. This is going to be the "feature set." Next, the column "Opportunity Result" from the *"sales_data"* data frame was used to develop a new data framework called "target."

The second phase in this stage is to separate the date frameworks into trainings and testing subsets using the steps below. Depending on the data set and desired predictions, it needs to be split into training and testing subset accordingly. For this exercise, we will use 75% of the data as training subset and rest 25% will be used for the testing subset. We will leverage the *"train_test_split()"* technique in "Scikit-Learn" to separate the data using steps and code as below:

Step 1 – To import required module, use command *"from sklearn.model_selection import train_test_split."*
Step 2 – To separate the data set, use command *"split data set into train and test setsdata_train, data_test,*

target_train, target_test = train_test_split (data,target, test_size = 0.30, random_state = 10)."

With the code above, the *"train_test_split"* module was first imported, followed by the use of *"train_test_split()"* technique to generate "training subset *(data_train, target_train)"* and "testing subset *(data_test, data_train)."* The *"train_test_split()"* technique's first argument pertains to the features that were divided in the preceding stage, the next argument relates to the target ("Opportunity Result"). The third "test size" argument is the proportion of the data we wish to divide and use as testing subset. We are using 30% for this example, although it can be any amount. The fourth 'random state' argument is used to make sure that the results can be reproduced every time.

Building the Machine Learning Model

The "machine_learning_map" provided by Scikit-Learn is widely used to choose the most appropriate ML algorithm for the data set. For this exercise, we will be using "Linear Support Vector Classification" and "K-nearest neighbors' classifier" algorithms.

Linear Support Vector Classification

"Linear Support Vector Classification" or "Linear SVC" is a sub-classification of "Support Vector Machine (SVM)" algorithm, which we have reviewed in the chapter 2 of this book titled "Machine Learning Algorithms." Using Linear SVC, the data can be divided into different planes so the algorithm can identify the optimal group structure for all the data classes.

Here are the steps and code for this algorithm to build our first ML model:

Step 1 – To import the required modules, use commands *"from sklearn.svm import LinearSVC"* and *"from sklearn.metrics import accuracy_score."*

Step 2 – To develop an LinearSVC object type, use command *"svc_model = LinearSVC (random_state=0)."*

Step 3 – To train the algorithm and generate predictions from the testing data, use command *"pred = svc_model.fit (data_train, target_train).predict (data_test)."*

Step 4 – To display the model accuracy score, use command *"print ('LinearSVC accuracy:,' accuracy_score (target_test, pred, normalize = True))."*

With the code above, the required modules were imported in the first step. We then developed a type of Linear SVC using *"svc_model"* object with "random_state" as '0.' The "random_state" command instructs the built-in random number generator to shuffle the data in a particular order. In step 3, the "Linear SVC" algorithm is trained on the training data set and subsequently used to generate predictions for the target from the testing data. The *"accuracy_score()"* technique was used in the end to verify the "accuracy score" of the model, which could be displayed as "LinearSVC accuracy : 0.777811004785," for instance.

K-Nearest Neighbors Classifier

The "k-nearest neighbors(k-NN)" algorithm is referred to as "a non-parametric method used for classification and regression in pattern recognition." In cases of classification and regression, "the input consists of the nearest k closest training examples in the feature space." K-NN is form of "instance-based learning," or "lazy learning," in which the function is only locally estimated, and all calculations are delayed until classification. The output is driven by the fact, whether the classification or regression method is used for k-NN:

- "k-nearest neighbors classification" - The "output" is a member of the class. An "object" is classified by its neighbors' plurality vote, assigning the object to the most prevalent class among its nearest "k-neighbors," where "k" denotes a small positive integer. If k= 1, the "object" is simply allocated to the closest neighbor's class.
- "k-nearest neighbors regression" - The output is the object's property value, which is computed as an average of the k-nearest neighbors values.

A helpful method for both classification and regression can be assigning weights to the neighbors' contributions, to allow closer neighbors to make more contributions in the average, compared to the neighbors located far apart. For instance, a known "weighting scheme" is to assign each neighbor a weight of "$1/d$," where "d" denotes the distance from the neighbor. The neighbors are selected from a set of objects for which the "class" (for "k-NN classification") or the feature value of the "object" (for "k-NN regression") is known.

Here are the steps and code for this algorithm to build our next ML model:

Step 1 – To import required modules, use command *"from sklearn.neighbors import KNeighborsClassifier"* and *"from sklearn.metrics import accuracy_score."*

Step 2 – To create object of the classifier, use command *"neigh = KNeighborsClassifier(n_neighbors=3)."*

Step 3 – To train the algorithm, use command *"neigh.fit(data_train, target_train)."*

Step 4 – To generate predictions, use command *"pred = neigh.predict(data_test)."*

Step 5 – To evaluate accuracy, use command *"print ('KNeighbors accuracy score:,' accuracy_score(target_test, pred))."*

With the code above, the required modules were imported in the first step. We then developed the object *"neigh"* of type "KNeighborsClassifier" with the volume of neighbors as *"n_neighbors=3."* In the next step, the *"fit()"* technique was used to train the algorithm on the training data set. Next, the model was tested on the testing data set using *"predict()"* technique. Finally, the accuracy score was obtained, which could be

"KNeighbors accuracy score : 0.814550580998," for instance.

Now that our preferred algorithms have been introduced, the model with the highest accuracy score can be easily selected. But wouldn't it be great if we had a way to compare the distinct models' efficiency visually? In Scikit-Learn, we can use the "Yellowbrick library," which offers techniques for depicting various scoring techniques visually.

Chapter 5: Training Neural Network with Tensorflow

TensorFlow can be defined as a Machine Learning platform providing end-to-end service with a variety of free and open sources. It has a system of multilayered nodes that allow for quick building, training and deployment of artificial neural networks with large data sets. It is touted as a "simple and flexible architecture to take new ideas from concept to code to state-of-the-art models and to publication at a rapid pace." For example, Google uses TensorFlow libraries in their image recognition and speech recognition tools and technologies.

Higher-level APIs such as "tf.estimator" can be used for specifying predefined architectures, such as "linear regressors" or "neural networks." The picture below shows existing hierarchy of the TensorFlow tool kit:

The picture shown below provides the purposes of the different layers:

Toolkit(s)	Description
Estimator (tf.estimator)	High-level, OOP API.
tf.layers/tf.losses/tf.metrics	Libraries for common model components.
TensorFlow	Lower-level APIs

The two fundamental components of TensorFlow are:
1. A "graph protocol buffer"
2. A "runtime" that can execute the graph

The two-component mentioned above are similar to "Python" code and the "Python interpreter." Just as "Python interpreter" can run Python code on several hardware systems, TensorFlow can be operated on various hardware systems, like CPU, GPU, and TPU.

To make a decision regarding which API(s) should be used, you must consider the API offering the highest abstraction level to solve the target problem. Easier to use, but (by design) less flexible, are the greater abstract levels. It is recommended to first begin with the highest-level API and make everything work. If for certain unique modelling issues, you need extra flexibility, move one level down. Notice that each level is constructed on the lower level APIs. It should thus be quite simple to decrease the hierarchy.

For the development of majority of Machine Learning models, we will use "tf.estimator" API, which significantly lowers the number of code lines needed for development. Also, "tf.estimator" is compatible with Scikit-Learn API.

Neural Network

The programming of computers needs a human programmer. Many lines of code are used by humans to instruct a computer to provide solutions to our problems.

However, the computer can attempt to fix the issue itself through machine learning and neural networks. A neural network is "a function that learns the expected output for a given input from training datasets." For instance, you can train the neural network with many sample bears pictures to construct a neural network that recognizes pictures of a bear. The resulting network operates as a functionality to generate the "bear" label as output for the bear picture input. Another more convenient example would be training the neural network using multiple user activity logs from gaming servers and generate an output stating which users are very likely to convert to paying customer.

Unlike the "Artificial Neural Network" (explained in detail in Chapter 2 of this book), the "Neural Network" features only a single neuron, also called as "perceptron." It is a straightforward and fundamental mechanism which can be implemented with basic math. The primary distinction between traditional programming and a neural network, is that computers running on neural network learn from the provided training data set to determine the parameters (weights and prejudice) on their own, without needing any human assistance. Algorithms like "back propagation" and "gradient descent" may be used to train the parameters. It can be stated that the computer tries to increase or decrease every parameter a bit, in the hope that the optimal combination of Parameters can be found, to minimize the error compared with training data set.

Fundamentals of Neural Network

- Neural networks need clear and informative big data to be trained. You can think of Neural networks as a toddler. They start by observing how their parents are walking. Then they attempt to walk on their own, and the kid learns how to accomplish future tasks with every step. Similarly, the Neural network may fail a few times, but it learns how to generate desired predictions after a few failing attempts.

- For complicated issues such as image processing, it is advisable to use Neural Networks. Neural networks belong to a group of algorithms called "representation learning algorithms." These algorithms are capable of simplifying complicated issues by generating simple (or "representative") form, which tends to be more difficult for conventional (non-representation) algorithms.

- To determine what type of neural network model is suitable for solving the issue at hand, let the data dictate how you fix the issue. For instance, "recurring neural networks" are more appropriate if the issue pertains to sequence generation. While it might be better for you to use "convolutional neural networks" to solve an image-related issue.

- In order to run a deep neural network model, hardware specifications are vital. Neural networks have been around for a long time now, but they are recently experiencing an upsurge primarily credited to the fact that computer resources today are better and more effective. If you want to address a real-life problem using neural network, it is wise to purchase high-end hardware.

Training a Neural Network Using TensorFlow

In this exercise we will develop a model of neural networks for classifying clothing images such as sneakers and shirts, using TensorFlow library.

I – Import the Dataset

For this example, we will be using "Fashion MNIST" data set with 60,000 pictures representing 10 different categories. The low-resolution pictures (28 to 28 pixels) indicate individual clothing items. For the classic MNIST dataset, "Fashion MNIST" is intended as a drop-in replacement. The "MNIST" data set includes pictures of handwritten numbers (0, 1, and so on.) in the same format as the clothing items used in this example. To train the network, we will use 60,000 pictures and 10,000 pictures will be used to assess the accuracy with which the network has learned how to classify pictures.

The "Fashion MNIST" data set is accessible directly from TensorFlow, using the import command as below:

"fashion_mnist = keras.datasets.fashion_mnist (train_images, train_labels), (test_images, test_labels) = fashion_mnist.load_data()"

After the dataset has been loaded system will return 4 different "NumPy arrays" including:

- The *"train_images"* and *"train_labels"* arrays, which serve as the "training dataset" for the model.
- The *"test_images"* and *"test_labels"* arrays, which serve as the "testing dataset" that the model can be tested against.'

Now we need to create labels for an array of integers (0 to 9), corresponding to each category/class of the clothing picture in the data set, using command below which will look like the table represented in the picture below. This will be useful in generating predictions using our model.

"class_names = ['T-shirt/top,' 'Trouser,' 'Pullover,' 'Dress,' 'Coat,' 'Sandal,' 'Shirt,' 'Sneaker,' 'Bag,' 'Ankle boot']"

Label	Class
0	T-shirt/top
1	Trouser
2	Pullover
3	Dress
4	Coat
5	Sandal
6	Shirt
7	Sneaker
8	Bag
9	Ankle boot

II – Data Exploration

To get some sense of the data set, it can be explored using commands listed below:

To view the total number of images in the "training data set" and the size of each image – "*train_images.shape*," which will produce the output displayed as "(60000, 28, 28)" stating we have 60,000 pictures of 28 to 28 pixel size.

To view the total number of labels in the "training dataset" – "*len(train_labels)*," which will produce the output displayed as "60000" stating we have 60,000 labels in the training data set.

To view the data type of each label used in the "training dataset"– "*train_labels*," which will produce the output displayed as "*array([9, 0, 0, ..., 3, 0, 5], dtype=uint8)*" stating each label is an integer between o and 9.

To view the total number of images in the "testing dataset" and the size of each image – "*test_images.shape*," which will produce the output displayed as "(10000, 28, 28)" stating we have 10,000 pictures of 28 to 28 pixel size in the testing data set.

To view the total number of labels in the "testing dataset" – "*len(test_labels)*," which will produce the output displayed as "10000" stating we have 10,000 labels in the testing data set.

III – Data Pre-Processing

To make the data suitable for training the model, it needs to be pre-processed. It is essential to pre-process the data sets to be used for training and testing in the same manner.

For instance, you notice the first picture in the training data set has the pixel values between 0 and 255, using the commands below:

"plt.figure()"

"plt.imshow(train_images[0])"

"plt.colorbar()"

"plt.grid(False)"

"plt.show()"

These pixel values need to be scaled to fall between 0 to 1, prior to being used as input for the Neural Network model. Therefore, the values need to be divided by 255, for both the data subsets, using commands below:

"train_images   =   train_images   /   255.0"

"test_images = test_images / 255.0"

The final pre-processing step here would be to make sure that the data is is desired format prior to building the Neural Network by viewing the first 20 pictures from the training dataset and displaying the "class name" under each picture, using commands below:

"plt.figure(figsize=(10,10))"

"for i in range(20):

   plt.subplot(5,5,i+1)

   plt.xticks([])

   plt.yticks([])

   plt.grid(False)

   plt.imshow(train_images[i], cmap=plt.cm.binary)

plt.xlabel(class_names[train_labels[i]])"

"plt.show()"

IV – Building the Neural Network Model

To build up the "Neural Network," the constituting layers of the model first need to be configured and only then the model can be compiled.

Configuring the Layers

The "layers" are the fundamental construction block of a neural network. These "layers" take out information from the data entered generating representations that tend to be extremely valuable addressing the problem.

Majority of "deep learning" involves stacking and linking fundamental layers together. The parameters that are learned during practice are available in most of the layers, like "tf.keras.layers.Dense." To configure the required layers, use command below:

"model = keras.Sequential([
    keras.layers.Flatten(input_shape=(28, 28)),
    keras.layers.Dense(128, activation=tf.nn.relu),
    keras.layers.Dense(10, activation=tf.nn.softmax)
])"

The "*tf.keras.layers.Flatten*" is the first layer in this network, which turns the picture format from a 2-dimesnional array of 28x28 size to a 1-dimension array with "28x28 = 784" pixels. Consider this layer as unchained rows of pixels in the picture that arranged these pictures but without any learning parameters and capable of only altering the data.

The network comprises of couple of "*tf.keras.layers.Dense*" layers after pixels are flattened. These are neural layers that are fully or densely connected. There are 128 nodes or neurons in the first Dense layer. The succeeding and final layer is a 10-node layer of "*Softmax*," which generated an array of ten different probability scores amounting to "1." Every single node includes a probability score indicating that one of the ten classes is likely to contain the existing picture.

Compiling the Model

Before being able to train the model, some final tweaks are needed to be made in the model compilation step, such as:

Loss function— This provides a measure of the model's accuracy during training. This feature should be minimized, so that the model is "directed" in the correct direction.

Optimizer —These are the updates made to the model on the basis of the data it can view as well as its "loss function."

Metrics — Used for monitoring the training and testing procedures. For example, the code below utilizes accuracy, measured by computing the fraction of the pictures that were classified accurately.

"model.compile(optimizer='adam,'

> *loss='sparse_categorical_crossentropy,'*
> *metrics=['accuracy'])"*

V – Training the Model

The steps listed below are used to train the "Neural Network Model":

- Feed the training data to the model, using *"train_images"* and *"train_labels"* arrays.

- Allow the network to learn association of pictures and corresponding labels.

- Generate predictions using the model for a predefined test date set, for example, the *"test_images"* array.   Then   the   predictions must   be   verified   by   matching   the   labels   from the *"test_labels"* array.

You   can   begin   to   train   the   network,   by   utilizing the *"model.fit"* method. To verify the systme is a "fit" for the   training   data,   use   command *"model.fit(train_images, train_labels, epochs=5)."*

The epochs are displayed as below, suggesting that the model has reached accuracy of around 0.89 or 89% of the training data:

"Epoch 1/5

60000/60000
[===============================] - 4s 75us/sample - loss: 0.5018 - acc: 0.8241

Epoch 2/5

60000/60000
[===============================] - 4s 71us/sample - loss: 0.3763 - acc: 0.8643

Epoch 3/5

60000/60000

[=============================] - 4s

71us/sample - loss: 0.3382 - acc: 0.8777

Epoch 4/5

60000/60000

[=============================] - 4s

72us/sample - loss: 0.3138 - acc: 0.8846

Epoch 5/5

60000/60000

[=============================] - 4s

72us/sample - loss: 0.2967 - acc: 0.8897

<tensorflow.python.keras.callbacks.History   at 0x7f65fb64b5c0>"

VI – Measuring the Accuracy of the Neural Network Model

To test the accuracy of the network, it must be verified against the testing data set using commands below:

"test_loss, test_acc = model.evaluate(test_images, test_labels)"

"print('Test accuracy:,' test_acc)"

The output can be obtained as shown below, which suggests that the accuracy of the test result is around 0.86 or 86%, which is slightly less that the accuracy of the training data set. This is a classic example of "overfitting," when the performance or accuracy of the model is lower on new input or testing data than the training data.

"10000/10000

[==============================] - 1s

51us/sample - loss: 0.3653 - acc: 0.8671

Test accuracy: 0.8671"

VII – Generate Predictions Using the Neural Network Model

Now that our model has been trained sufficiently, we are ready to generate predictions from the model, using command *"predictions = model.predict(test_images)."*

In the code below, the network has generated a prediction for labels of each picture in the testing data set. The prediction is generated as an array of ten integers with the "confidence" index for each of the ten categories (refer the import data stage) corresponding to the the test picture.

"predictions[0]"

"array([6.58371528e-06, 1.36480646e-10, 4.17183337e-08, 1.15178166e-10,

8.30939484e-07, 1.49914682e-01, 3.11488043e-06, 4.63472381e-02,

6.10820061e-05, 8.03666413e-01], dtype=float32)"

To view the label with the highest "confidence" index, using command *"np.argmax (predictions[0])."*

A result "9," will suggest that the model has maximum confidence on the test image belonging to *"class_names[9]"* or according to our labels table, ankle boot. To verify this prediction, use command *"test_labels[0],"* which should generate output as "9."

To view the whole set of predictions for the ten classes, use command below:

"def plot_image(i, predictions_array, true_label, img):
  predictions_array, true_label, img =
predictions_array[i], true_label[i], img[i]
  plt.grid(False)
  plt.xticks([])
  plt.yticks([])

```
plt.imshow(img, cmap=plt.cm.binary)


predicted_label = np.argmax(predictions_array)
if predicted_label == true_label:
  color = 'blue'
else:
  color = 'red'


plt.xlabel('{} {:2.0f}%
({}).'format(class_names[predicted_label],
                  100*np.max(predictions_array),
                  class_names[true_label]),
                  color=color)


def plot_value_array(i, predictions_array, true_label):
  predictions_array, true_label = predictions_array[i],
true_label[i]
  plt.grid(False)
  plt.xticks([])
  plt.yticks([])
  thisplot = plt.bar(range(10), predictions_array,
color='#777777')
  plt.ylim([0, 1])
  predicted_label = np.argmax(predictions_array)
```

thisplot[predicted_label].set_color('red')

thisplot[true_label].set_color('blue')"

Now, for example, you may want to generate a prediction for a specific picture in the testing data set. You can do this using the command below:

"Grab an image from the test dataset
img = test_images[0]
print(img.shape)"

"(28, 28)"

To use the "tf.keras" models to generate this prediction, the picture must be added to a list, since these models have been optimized to generate predictions on a "collection of dataset" at a time. Use command below to accomplish this:

"# Add the image to a batch where it's the only member.
img = (np.expand_dims(img,0))

print(img.shape)"

"(1, 28, 28)"

Now, to generate the prediction for the picture using "tf.keras" use the command below:

"predictions_single = model.predict(img)
print(predictions_single)"

The predictions generated will resemble the code below:

"[[6.5837266e-06 1.3648087e-10 4.1718483e-08
1.1517859e-10 8.3093937e-07

  1.4991476e-01 3.1148918e-06 4.6347316e-02
6.1082108e-05 8.0366623e-01]]"

To generate a graph or plot for the prediction (as shown in the picture below), use command below:

*"plot_value_array(0, predictions_single, test_labels)
plt.xticks(range(10), class_names, rotation=45)
plt.show()"*

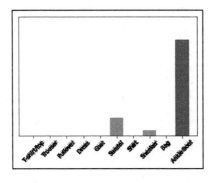

The *"model.predict"* generated the output as a "list of lists," for every single picture in the testing data set. To generate predictions specifically for the specific image we used earlier, use command below:

"prediction_result = np.argmax(predictions_single[0]) print(prediction_result)"

The output or prediction generated should be "9" as we obtained earlier.

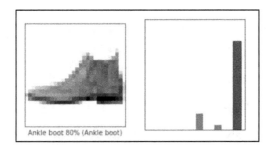

Ankle boot 80% (Ankle boot)

Python Tips and Tricks for Developers

Python was first implemented in 1989 and is regarded as highly user-friendly and simple to learn programming language for entry level coders and amateurs. It is regarded ideal for individuals newly interested in programming or coding and need to comprehend programming fundamentals. This stems from the fact that Python reads almost the same as English language. Therefore, it requires less time to understand how the language works and focus can be directed in learning the basics of programming.

Python is an interpreted language that supports automatic memory management and object-oriented programming. This extremely intuitive and flexible programming language can be used for coding projects such as: machine learning algorithms, web applications, data mining and visualization, game development.

Some of the tips and tricks you can leverage to sharpen up your Python programming skill set are:

In-place swapping of two numbers:

"x, y = 100, 200
print(x, y)
x, y = y, x
print(x, y)"

Resulting Output =
100 200
200 100

Reversing a string:

```
a ="machine"
print("Reverse is," a[::-1])
```

Resulting Output =
Reverse is enihcam.

Creating a single string from multiple list elements:

```
a = ["machine," "learning," "algorithms"]
print(" .".join(a))
```

Resulting Output =
machine learning algorithms

Stacking of comparison operators:

```
n = 10
result = 1 < n < 20
print(result)
result = 1 > n <= 9
print(result)
```

Resulting Output =
True
False

Print the file path of the imported modules:

"import os;

import socket;

print(os)

print(socket"

Resulting Output =

"<module 'os' from '/usr/lib/python3.5/os.py'>

<module 'socket' from '/usr/lib/python3.5/socket.py'>"

Use of enums in Python:

"class MyName:

Geeks, For, Geeks = range(3)

print(MyName.Geeks)

print(MyName.For)

print(MyName.Geeks)"

Resulting Output =

2

1

2

Return multiple values from functions:

"def x():

return 1, 2, 3, 4

a, b, c, d = x()

print(a, b, c, d)"

Resulting Output =

"1 2 3 4"

Identify the value with highest frequency:

"test = [1, 2, 3, 4, 2, 2, 3, 1, 4, 4, 4]

print(max(set(test), key = test.count))"

Resulting Output =

4

Check the memory usage of an object:

"import sys

x = 1

print(sys.getsizeof(x))"

Resulting Output =

28

Printing a string N times:

"n = 2;

a ="machinelearning";

*print(a * n);"*

Resulting Output =

machinelearningmachinelearningmachinelearning

Identify anagrams:

"from collections import Counter

def is_anagram(str1, str2):

*   return Counter(str1) == Counter(str2)*

print(is_anagram('geek,' 'eegk'))

print(is_anagram('geek,' 'peek'))"

Resulting Output =

True

False

Transposing a matrix:

"mat = [[1, 2, 3], [4, 5, 6]]

*zip(*mat)"*

Resulting Output =

[(1, 4), (2, 5), (3, 6)]

Print a repeated string without using loops:

*"print "machine"*3+' '+"learning"*4"*

Resulting Output =
Machinemachinemachine
learninglearninglearninglearning

Measure the code execution time:

"import time"
"startTime = time.time()"
" write your code or functions calls"
" write your code or functions calls"

"endTime = time.time()"
"totalTime = endTime – startTime"
"print('Total time required to execute code is=' , totalTime)"

Resulting Output =
Total time

Obtain the difference between two lists:

"list1 = ['Scott,' 'Eric,' 'Kelly,' 'Emma,' 'Smith']
list2 = ['Scott,' 'Eric,' 'Kelly']
set1 = set(list1)

set2 = set(list2)

list3 = list(set1.symmetric_difference(set2))

print(list3)"

Resulting Output =

list3 = ['Emma,' 'Smith]

Calculate the memory being used by an object in Python:

"import sys"

"list1 = ['Scott,' 'Eric,' 'Kelly,' 'Emma,' 'Smith']"

"print("size of list = ,"sys.getsizeof(list1))"

"name = 'pynative.com'"

"print('size of name =' ,sys.getsizeof(name))"

Resulting Output =

('size of list = ,' 112)

('size of name = ,' 49)

Removing duplicate items from the list:

"listNumbers = [20, 22, 24, 26, 28, 28, 20, 30, 24]"

"print ('Original=' , listNumbers)"

"listNumbers = list(set(listNumbers))"

"print ('After removing duplicate= ' , listNumbers)"

Resulting Output =

"'Original= ,' [20, 22, 24, 26, 28, 28, 20, 30, 24]"

"'After removing duplicate= ,' [20, 22, 24, 26, 28, 30]"

Find if a list contains identical elements:

"listOne = [20, 20, 20, 20]

print('All element are duplicate in listOne,'

listOne.count(listOne[0]) == len(listOne))

listTwo = [20, 20, 20, 50]

print('All element are duplicate in listTwo,'

listTwo.count(listTwo[0]) == len(listTwo))"

Resulting Output =

"'All element are duplicate in listOne,' True"

"'All element are duplicate in listTwo,' False"

Efficiently compare two unordered lists:

"from collections import Counter

one = [33, 22, 11, 44, 55]

two = [22, 11, 44, 55, 33]

print('is two list are b equal,' Counter(one) ==

Counter(two))"

Resulting Output =

"'is two list are b equal,' True"

Check if list contains all unique elements:

"def isUnique(item):

tempSet = set()

return not any(i in tempSet or tempSet.add(i) for i in item)

listOne = [123, 345, 456, 23, 567]

print('All List elements are Unique' , isUnique(listOne))

listTwo = [123, 345, 567, 23, 567]

print('All List elements are Unique' , isUnique(listTwo))"

Resulting Output =

"All List elements are Unique True"

"All List elements are Unique False"

Convert Byte into String:

"byteVar = b"pynative""

"str = str(byteVar.decode('utf-8'))"

"print('Byte to string is' , str)"

Resulting Output =

"Byte to string is pynative"

Merge two dictionaries into a single expression:

"currentEmployee = {1: 'Scott,' 2: 'Eric,' 3:'Kelly'}

formerEmployee = {2: 'Eric,' 4: 'Emma'}

```
def merge_dicts(dictOne, dictTwo):
dictThree = dictOne.copy()
dictThree.update(dictTwo)
return dictThree
print(merge_dicts(currentEmployee,
formerEmployee))"
```

Conclusion

Thank you for making it through to the end of *Learn Python: The Ultimate Beginner's Guide to Python for Machine Learning and Deep Learning Using scikit-learn and tensorflow with Hands-On Projects*; let's hope it was informative and able to provide you with all of the tools you need to achieve your goals whatever they may be.

The next step is to make the best use of your newfound wisdom in today's cutting-edge technologies, primarily machine learning, that have created the "Silicon Valley" powerhouse. Today, machine learning technology has given rise to sophisticated machines, which can study human behavior and activity in order to recognize fundamental patterns of human behavior and exactly predict which products and services consumer may be interested in. Under the façade of their business model, businesses with an eye for the future are gradually become technology firms with systems built upon machine learning algorithms. Consider some of the most innovative tech gadgets of this era such as "Amazon Alexa," "Apple's Siri" and "Google Home," what they all have in common is their underlying machine learning capabilities. Now that you have finished reading this book and mastered the use of Scikit-Learn and TensorFlow libraries, you are all set to start developing your own Python machine learning model using all the open sources readily available and explicitly mentioned in this book for that purpose. You can position yourself to use your deep knowledge and understanding of machine learning technologies obtained from this book to contribute to the growth of any company and land yourself a new high paying and rewarding job!

Finally, if you found this book useful in any way, a review on Amazon is always appreciated!

www.ingramcontent.com/pod-product-compliance
Lightning Source LLC
LaVergne TN
LVHW051235050326
832903LV00028B/2422